Accessible Vacations

Accessible Vacations

An Insider's Guide to 12 US Cities

Simon J. Hayhoe

ROWMAN & LITTLEFIELD
Lanham • Boulder • New York • London

Published by Rowman & Littlefield
An imprint of The Rowman & Littlefield Publishing Group, Inc.
4501 Forbes Boulevard, Suite 200, Lanham, Maryland 20706
https://rowman.com

6 Tinworth Street, London SE11 5AL, United Kingdom

British Library Cataloguing in Publication Information Available

Library of Congress Cataloging-in-Publication Data

Names: Hayhoe, Simon, author.
Title: Accessible vacations : an insider's guide to 12 US cities / Simon J.
    Hayhoe.
Description: Lanham : Rowman & Littlefield, [2020] | Includes
    bibliographical references and index.
Identifiers: LCCN 2020001691 (print) | LCCN 2020001692 (ebook) | ISBN
    9781538128695 (cloth) | ISBN 9781538128701 (epub)
Subjects: LCSH: People with disabilities--Travel--United
    States--Guidebooks.
Classification: LCC HV1568.6 .H39 2020 (print) | LCC HV1568.6 (ebook) |
    DDC 917.304/933087--dc23
LC record available at https://lccn.loc.gov/2020001691
LC ebook record available at https://lccn.loc.gov/2020001692

♾ ™ The paper used in this publication meets the minimum requirements of American National Standard for Information Sciences Permanence of Paper for Printed Library Materials, ANSI/NISO Z39.48-1992.

Contents

Chapter One

Introduction

Everyone has the right freely to participate in the cultural life of the community, to enjoy the arts and to share in scientific advancement and its benefits.[1]
—Article 27 of the Universal Declaration of Human Rights

Accessible Vacations is a problem-solving guide book written to give you an informed choice of the most accessible museums, monuments, and theaters for vacation visits or day trips. It plants the seeds for accessible outings, activities, courses, and exhibitions you may want to try out, as well as places to go see great shows or movies.

Accessible Vacations is not an exhaustive list and won't try to sell you a hotel room or a flight. It also won't tell you about diners in the local area or the best souvenirs. It's written in the hope of making your life easier and more interesting in your leisure time. It also gives you a realistic, accessible picture of what's available in the US when you choose your destinations.

Whether it's viewing paintings, watching musicals, or even traveling up tall buildings, you can learn, find pleasure, develop personal interests, and build a life journey in US cities. You just need to know where to go to make these activities possible, and how cultural places can help support elderly people and people with sensory and intellectual access needs.

It is written in honor of your spirit of adventure.

MY FIRST EXPERIENCE OF TRAVELING
THROUGH THE US

To know how the intimate experiences in this book came about, you've got to understand how my early travels informed it.

My first view of the US coast to coast was from the window of a Greyhound bus.

In 1991, when I was in my early twenties, I had a student internship at a university in Vancouver, Canada. I was short of cash at the time, so I relied on a four-day pass to travel from New York City to Vancouver via Greyhound, crossing the border to Canada just after passing through Seattle and the Puget Sound.

I spent weeks before the trip poring over the Greyhound timetable, a thick book in those days that was like a literary atlas of the US and almost as thick as a local telephone directory. After ploughing through the timetable, I found a passage of travel with minimum stops that would, given luck, take me from East to West seaboards in just under four days. The only downside to this plan was that it would mean starting at New York's Port Authority Bus Station at midnight.

For those who didn't know New York back then, in the early 1990s the city wasn't the city it is today. I always think wistfully about those times when I pass through the modern, safer Port Authority and linger to buy a juice or grab a cup of coffee.

In those days, you didn't stop at the Port Authority long if you could help it. As soon as you got into the building, hustlers would try to snatch your bag, pretending to provide you with a cheap service for a small tip. From there, you could be taken down a corridor and held up with a knife or a pistol.

Despite running the gauntlet to get to my bay, a few minutes to midnight I put my bag in the hold of the first bus of the new day and settled into my first sticky bus seat. This and two other Greyhound seats were to be my home for the next three and three-quarter days. I slept often on that trip, but I have rarely felt so tired since.

On the road, I had a completely different experience of the US. The first big city I passed through was Philadelphia, the original grand, industrial city of the country, with its historic buildings and port on the wide Delaware River. Then it was on to Chicago, the giant of the Midwest, all skyscrapers and Great Lakes so long and wide they were more like oceans—in those days the Sears Tower was still the tallest skyscraper in the world.

Further into the Midwest, I took a break in Minneapolis-Saint Paul, the twin cities, where I stocked up on provisions. Close to the Greyhound station, I saw a club with the names of bands who'd played there on plates around the outside wall—Prince (of course) and Motorhead (more of a surprise)—which made me promise myself to return one day and take a closer look.

From Minneapolis, I traveled further west, where the cities got smaller and farther apart, like the staging-posts of Bismarck in North Dakota and Miles City in Montana. At first, I thought these places were sets from 1950s Western movies, with ranchers wearing ten-gallon hats and holstered guns.

After the vast Midwest, it was over the Rockies and Cascades by day and night, and then on to the West Coast and Seattle, a surprisingly exciting city surrounded by coastal mountains. This was the first time I'd seen the Pacific, which seemed as cold as the Atlantic coast but blue-greener and shimmery.

The houses were different again on this Pacific coastline. More interestingly, the teenagers wore very different, grungier-looking clothes and had wilder hair from those I'd known back East.

I learned two things from this journey.

The first thing I learned was that the US has a rich, beautiful history and culture. It's a place of natural exquisiteness and wide-open spaces. It also has exciting cities, big and small, founded on commerce and governments, roads and railways, education and religion.

US cities nurture and attract famous painters, sculptors and actors, philanthropists and writers. They also attract people from all over the world to work and develop new trades, which gives these cities cultural depth—Little Italys and Chinatowns, Korea Towns and French Quarters are now almost as synonymous as skyscrapers and four-lane highways in most of the US's biggest cities.

I also noticed that the US has always been culturally diverse. From state to state, coast to coast, north to south, its states of mind have evolved according to its environment and migration.

The US doesn't just have different peoples, different attitudes, different states of mind, different buildings, and different heritage. It's all those things and more—it's not just one country, it's half a continent of many countries. Its whole can be said to be bigger than the sum of its parts, and so its culture can be said to have many, many possibilities.

This first journey, then, became my Grand Tour of the US, a journey equivalent to the ones the wealthy would take around the elegant ruins of Italy and Greece in the eighteenth and nineteenth centuries.

The journey not only taught me about the early settlers to the US and what they saw as they traveled west after independence. It taught me about the history of a country that helped forge the modern world from industry, commerce, transport, and wealth.

It's not surprising that US cities are a magnet for modern cultural visits, and cultural places are among their most important landmarks. Many of these cultural places were founded in the nineteenth century and early twentieth centuries, in a period when the US was growing rapidly and finding its place in the world.

This was a time when its modern legends were being acted out.

Visiting these cities as cultural centers is one of the major reasons people from the US and all over the world travel to and throughout the country—these places are equally popular among traveling Americans and international tourists alike.

The second thing I learned on this journey, and something that has become more obvious the older I get and the more I keep traveling, is that cities are difficult to get to and just as hard to get around.

In my early twenties, it was a tough journey. And when I got off the bus, it was difficult to know where I wanted to go, to get where I wanted to go, to find information, to find the right person to talk to, even to find my next bus. For a more infirm person, a person with learning difficulties, or a person with a loss of sight, hearing, mobility, or memory, this task becomes harder still.

Of course, traveling on Greyhounds isn't everybody's idea of a vacation, even those who are the most mobile and those with the sharpest limbs, hearing, and sight. What's more, accessibility in the US has moved on markedly since this journey, and it has become more manageable for older people and for people who find it difficult to see, hear, or get around.

But like any other country in the world, the US can be a confusing and less accessible place if you find it difficult to do these things.

ACCESSIBILITY AND THE LAW

Legislation has helped visitors with all kinds of needs to get access to cultural places in the US. Importantly, my journey in 1991 was less than a year after the first access legislation for US citizens was introduced, the Americans with Disabilities Act (which is now known as the ADA), on July 26, 1990.

Whether you think of yourself as disabled or not, this legislation was a game changer for access. Although after this bill was passed, it took many years to become effective and we are only starting to see its most important changes now.

Importantly, the ADA and similar laws elsewhere helped to change attitudes of people like me and the people I work with in education and cultural places around the world. It made us think about how we used computers and other technologies, how we provided public education, how we built or changed building spaces, and how we developed information for the public. Importantly, it also legitimized making places accessible and helped us make a case for access and inclusion to event and educational managers, theatrical directors, and museum curators.

But one thing the ADA couldn't do was to let cultural visitors with access needs know how to access the places they wanted to visit. It also couldn't help people know what accessible options they had when planning their vacations and day trips.

To put it another way, the ADA couldn't educate the public about what was out there for them, how to get to their local cultural places, what technologies they could find once they got to these places, and what learning opportunities were available when they got there.

What I've learned in my work with arts education and cultural visits for more than twenty-five years is that it's the little things that make it hard for visitors to go on vacation or take a day trip.

That is to say, the things that put potential visitors off most from going on vacation or day trips are what seem to be overlooked in their planning. It is the fear of climbing down into dark subway stations. It is not knowing the right people to ask for the correct transportation. It is not knowing who to trust for help on your journeys. It is not knowing the right people to talk to in cultural places so your visit is interesting and entertaining, and not knowing the people who can communicate with you. It is not knowing where to look to make a tour, a play, a musical, or a movie a memorable event.

What this first edition of *Accessible Vacations* does is tell you what is available in the US cities that I feel are the most interesting, exciting, and accessible cities to visit. It tells you the most accessible areas of these cities and how you can make your visits fulfilling and comfortable.

Importantly, it shows where you can find information to educate yourself about your own access and gain added value from your visit.

ACCESSIBLE VACATIONS'S FIVE-STEP PLAN

During my early studies on adult education and cultural visits by people with access needs, I heard what visitors felt was important and watched how they took part in courses, exhibitions, and shows. From these studies, I formulated a simple plan for making access easier and less burdensome based on my research with groups of younger and older visitors.

This simple plan was then made into a five-step plan for making the most of cultural places. This five-step plan is based on observations I made from talking to visitors and going with them on their visits. These observations were then recorded in my books *Arts, Culture, and Blindness*,[2] *Blind Visitor Experiences at Art Museums*,[3] and *Cultural Heritage, Ageing, Disability, and Identity*.[4]

The first observation was that there is no such thing as a *type* of person with an access need. Individual hard-of-hearing people aren't like all other hard-of-hearing people; individual people with sight problems aren't like all other people with sight problems.

Even if people use canes to walk or wheelchairs to get around, they do so in their own unique way. We are who we are mostly from our needs and wants, some coming from when we were children, others coming from our adult experiences with other people we like to be with—whether it's the people we're raised with or the family we've chosen and are raising later in life.

Most importantly, the family you come from, the lessons your parents taught you, and the arts you were encouraged to do at home are far more important than your access needs when it comes to cultural visits. These parts of the jigsaw puzzle of your past do so much to determine what you like doing nowadays.

The second observation was that some people like to visit with other people with the same access needs as theirs, while others prefer only to visit with visitors without access needs.

There is good news for these people, as most cultural places have options for different sets of needs. These places have tours, performances, and classes for people with access needs. They also have ways of helping people with access needs to enjoy the main performances or tours, so audiences can sit with their friends or families without access needs. There is also often a kind of halfway house where people can sit in a main performance where there are people with and without access needs, or sit with others who have their same needs.

The third observation was that technology may have changed and people can visit museums virtually, but people still like to visit in person even if it is uncomfortable to do so. This observation was clearest in a study of visitors with sight problems to the Metropolitan Museum of Art, New York, that I led in 2011.

In this Metropolitan study, I interviewed visitors who had visual impairments and who could have stayed at home and discovered artworks on the museum's website, saving time and money. Instead, I observed that visitors would rather brave New York's subways, with no local stop to the museum, or the city buses, special buses, or taxis to actually *be* in the museum.

From this study, I found that people prefer to visit museums and be next to a painting or sit in a theater and experience a performance than watch it, hear it, or read about it at home. It is the feeling of "being there" that counts as part of experiencing culture rather than seeing the picture and reading about these artworks in the comfort of their home.

The fourth and perhaps most important observation was that people don't feel like visiting cultural places unless they feel they can gain something from them. This observation became so important that I even once did a public lecture titled, "Is Belief More Important Than Ability in the Visual Arts?"

This lecture was based on a study I conducted of arts students in a school for the blind in the early 2000s, who were learning about their subject in class and through visits. In this study, I found students seemed to be one of two types: the first type did art enthusiastically because they were told they were capable of doing so early in childhood; the second type avoided their studies because they were told they were incapable of doing so as young children.

What was more, no matter what was done to teach these students, and no matter how much we told these students they were able to do art, the students who were told they were incapable still believed what they were told as children.

These observations led me to identify five of the most important things people need when they visit cultural places, which I developed into a stepped plan.[5] These five things are as follows:

1. Visiting with people you know or feel comfortable around—that is to say, the chance to *bond*
2. *Learning* about your culture or someone else's culture when you get to your cultural place
3. *Information and technology* that's available from cultural places, how to get to them and around them, and information about the pieces of art or performances once you get there
4. Access to *spaces and places* when you visit cultural places
5. Ease of *mobility*, of both getting there and getting around cultural places

The following chapters of *Accessible Vacations* will bear in mind these five things, showing you the most important parts of your visit. This will help you break down and plan your visit more effectively. What is more, the research for *Accessible Vacations* has focused on gathering information using these five steps.

WHAT FOLLOWS IN *ACCESSIBLE VACATIONS*

Accessible Vacations is in two main sections, designed to show you what access is out there for you, the technologies you can access, and the best means for you to access your visits.

Section I—Access Needs

This section includes chapters on ways you can get access to museums and theaters if you have problems with seeing, hearing, memory, or learning. These ways can include technologies, audio descriptions, captions, special classes and performances, sign language, and accessible mobile technologies.

Section II—Twelve Cities

This section has a chapter each for a dozen differently styled big, accessible US cities, with listings of facilities for museums and theaters according to this book's five-step method of finding information. These cities were chosen because they are among the most visited in the US, they are spread throughout the country, and they are the home of important cultural places that represent this country so well. They are also a mix of young and old cities, centers of the arts, different forms of art, and centers of business. They include the East and West seaboards and the states of the North and South as well as the Midwest. So, no matter what you're looking for in a vacation, there should be something here for you.

This second section, as the title of this book suggests, features twelve highly visited cities in the US from a wide choice of locations. I have curated these sections not just to choose the most visited cities but also to provide a spread of old and new, theater and fine art, and representations of different state cultures.

From the Southern states, I've chosen Miami, Atlanta, and Houston. These cities represent New South culture, plus they are modern but surrounded by old, traditional, and important states. Miami is well known for its clean, white beaches, glass and steel skyscrapers, and bright-colored art-deco architecture and Cuban community. Atlanta was founded as a railway town and is another relatively young, confident, business-oriented city in an old rural state with a strong history. By contrast, as I write Houston is the fourth-largest city in the US, has a vibrant arts scene, and has a combination of Hispanic and contemporary US culture shaped by its own complex history.

From the Western states, I chose Seattle, Los Angeles, and San Francisco. These cities are iconic cities of the arts, have their own distinct cultures, and often represent the US to the rest of the world. Known for its highly distinctive arts scene, culture, and gorgeous surroundings, Seattle is one of the most beautiful big cities to visit in the US. In many ways, Los Angeles is perhaps the most iconic city in the West of the US, known the world over for the movies and great personal wealth which has spawned great art foundations. Although not too far north of Los Angeles, San Francisco looks more traditional with its old-style architecture, seemingly never-ending hills, spectacular views, and of course its technology.

Like my choices from the Western states, I chose my cities from the Eastern states—New York; Washington, DC; Philadelphia; and Boston—for their distinct and distinguished cultures. Importantly, and for very different reasons, each of these Eastern cities represents the US to the rest of the world, and also represents the original large cities of what became the US. As the largest and perhaps most identifiable city in the Eastern US, New York is an icon of the country to the rest of the world, with its recognizable monuments, theaters, and fine arts. In a quieter way, Washington, DC, is the cultural heartbeat of the US as a whole, with its traditional architecture, the official home of the US government, and the home of national culture. In the early nineteenth century, Philadelphia, developed on its port on the Delaware River, was the largest city in the US and the original large city in the US, known for its magnificent architecture and commerce. If Washington, DC, can be seen as the guardian of national culture, Boston can be seen as the home of US philosophy, with its historical universities, understated architecture, and early Atlantic port.

To know the "real America," you have to know the Midwest, and from this part of the US I have chosen the interesting and characteristic Chicago and Denver to visit. Chicago is a vast city with a fascinating mix of industry, early and late twentieth-century architecture, canals, and jazz heritage, all set on the shores of a lake so vast that you can't see its farthest shores. Last, as the highest large city in the US, Denver has clean air, stunning views of the night stars, and panoramic views of the Rockies, and retains a character of its founding Western pioneers.

Finally, a word about what this book can't do. Although I've done my best to give you the most up-to-date information and advice to plan your journey, it should be kept in mind that cities, websites, programs, and even museums and theaters change—and sometimes they even close. It's important to think of this book as a starting point, one that needs a little checking on your part before you leave to see if, for example, accessible courses are still running and institutional opening times are still the same. It should also be borne in mind that services change for historical and financial reasons, so please make sure the service you want to use still exists in the form it is described, or still exists at all.

Section I

Access Needs

This section is written for people with sight or hearing loss or difficulties with learning. It is also for professionals who work with visitors, audiences, or classes with these losses or difficulties. It's written to provide an overview of access needs and show what can be done to help ameliorate the effects of these access needs during visits to cultural places.

If you're a person with an access need, I hope to reassure you that you're not alone and many other people often have the same issues as you. In this section, I'll also show you ways of managing your access needs and tell you about some well-known techniques and technologies to make visiting easier. Reading this book will be like peeking behind a stage curtain and seeing all the behind-the-scenes departments working toward creating an enjoyable show.

For professionals who are thinking of making their cultural places more accessible, this section provides an overview and support techniques to help you begin the process. Again, these aren't an exhaustive list of techniques, but they are among the most well-worn paths for developing access.

DEVELOPING ACCESS OR PLANNING YOUR OWN ACCESS

I begin this section on access techniques by developing the points I raised in the first chapter. Developing access in cultural places needs to overcome several key problems—whether you're a person trying to get access or a professional trying to provide it.

The first issue is the need to challenge the belief that the ability to learn or enjoy the arts is based on the ability to see, hear, remember, read, talk, or write. It's important to emphasize that the ability to gain something out of cultural places is purely an issue of the mind and the emotions—just as falling in love is not a matter of ability or intelligence either.

That is to say, you can enjoy doing something even if you don't have the ability to see, hear, remember, or even tell other people about your experience.

Some of the greatest artists, whose paintings hang in our most prestigious museums and galleries, did not have the full use of their sight and hearing when they created their art. Some of our most famous composers, performers, musicians, and actors also had problems with memory, reading, writing, and hearing.

Famously, Monet had sight loss when he was painting the last of his Water Lilies Series. Beethoven was deaf as he aged and composed some of his most well-known symphonies, as was Goya when he painted his most famous works on the French invasion of Spain. These amazing artists show that even though it may take a little more time to plan or attend a visit or a performance due to an access need, the fulfilment when you get there is still the same as anyone else's.

In my experience of cultural heritage, the biggest barrier I've found is challenging the belief that not all people get something out of their culture or the culture of others. Of course, it should be emphasized that it isn't normally the fault of the professionals who work in cultural places that this attitude exists. It is also certainly not the fault of people who believe they can't understand works of art. Quite the opposite.

I've always found that changing beliefs is a matter of educating yourself about the nature of hearing and sight problems and learning difficulties.

The second issue is that people with access needs are usually assumed to be like people who have lost all sight or hearing, or who have a complete inability to remember, read, or even talk.

For instance, when I first started working on cultural access, people with sight loss were only offered Braille labels or a few objects they could touch when they visited a museum. What's more, and as I pointed out in the first chapter, if visitors with sight problems were offered a description of artworks, these descriptions rarely spoke about color or shade.

This attempt to hide or deny *visual* things to people with sight loss—and even to deny the people who have never seen the chance to learn about sight—was often caused by a belief that people with sight problems would be offended by vision or had less ability to understand what was being said.

Many people who developed access in the old days were also taught that people with sight problems couldn't understand the visual world intellectually as well as people with full sight. As with the first issue, there was a general assumption that intellectual ability was based on the ability to see, hear, read, write, and remember.[1]

Research on this issue and the research of others has shown this assumption is wrong.[2] People with even some remaining sight will rely on their vision, and even people who are born without sight can understand visual things such as color, foreground, and background.

And so, instead of denying people with access needs the right to know about the world around them, we need to think of access needs in two different types. These types are based on my previous work with visual problems.

The first types of access needs are those based on the severity of issues that can prevent people from gaining full access to cultural places, performances, or exhibitions. These needs are of three kinds.

The first kind of needs are what I call *holistic needs*, or needs that affect a whole visit, such as not being able to see or hear at all, or being unable to write or speak at all. This kind of need means people will often want a completely different way of learning, speaking, writing, or reading, such as Braille or sign language—in other words, people with these needs will need a wholly different way of understanding, sensing, and communicating with the world. Holistic needs may mean you can communicate through a machine or pictures rather than speaking or reading from paper.

The second kind of needs are *substantial needs*, such as being able to see but not make out a person's face, or being able to hear but not being able to hear words. These needs make accessing cultural places difficult, but people with this kind of need can communicate ideas and have ideas communicated using adapted regular methods. For instance, museum visitors with substantial needs may be able to see a painting if a photonegative image of it is taken, or musical-goers may be able to hear the rhythm of music but not the words. Similarly, people with these needs may be able to communicate in spoken sentences but unable to read or write them.

The third kind of needs are *partial needs*, such as being able to recognize a person's face but not being able to see details or hearing speech but missing some words. These access needs may also include difficulties with reading and writing, concentrating for long periods, or reading passages of text. For instance, people with partial needs may be people who can communicate their ideas but find reading and writing those ideas difficult. Similarly, museum visitors with these access needs may find it easy to get to cultural places and use the mainstream facilities, but they may find it difficult to access a performance or an artwork.

The second types of access needs are those based on the age at which people first need support. These types of access needs are often overlooked, but they are just as important because they make a difference to people's education, experiences of culture throughout their life, and even their confidence. If it's related to sensory perception, an access need may also relate to understanding what hearing or seeing has ever been. As with the first type, these access needs are also of three kinds.

The first kind includes those who are born with access needs or who develop their access need before the age of three or four—there is no hard and fast rule, as people often develop at different ages when they're very young. My own studies show the key to this issue is that people with access needs have gone through their earliest years, grown up, and learned technologies to support their needs.

For instance, because of the nature of learning disabilities, people are more likely to be born with a particular type of need, such as people who find reading difficult. These people have never experienced reading and so have spent their entire lives relying more on spoken descriptions and more recently multimedia.

Similarly, museum visitors without sight in the first four years of life will mostly be taught Braille when they are older and be taught with fewer visual references at school. Consequently, these visitors will most likely appreciate Braille labeling when they go to museums and not appreciate visual information—not because they can't understand it, but because they've been taught they can't understand it or have little use for it.

What's more, members of audiences at theaters or museums who were born with little or no hearing will similarly be more likely to learn sign language and not rely on spoken language. Consequently, when these audience members attend an exhibition tour, a play, a concert, a musical, or an opera, they will appreciate a signer or interpreter during the performance.

The second kind of age-based access need occurs when people are assimilated to these needs when they are young, but later on have memories of not having needs. Generally speaking, the visitors who have these access needs acquired them in their mid-to-late childhood or even in adolescence or early adulthood, often between the ages of four and eighteen. Although, as with all these things, there are again no hard and fast rules.

Consequently, visitors with these access needs may choose to go to cultural places in separate groups or with friends and family. What's more, visitors with these needs are more likely to want a combination of ways of getting around and understanding works of art.

For example, theater and museum visitors with hearing problems that developed in late childhood will have experienced talking, even if they do not hear their voice or others' voices. However, these visitors will probably have learned sign language, even if they have been to regular schools or mixed with children who hear. Similarly, people with sight loss that developed in late childhood will understand the visual world around them from direct experience, but they also will be used to Braille and different technologies.

The third kind of age-based access need occurs in visitors who developed access needs in adulthood, especially old age. Although these are generally the people who are least considered by cultural places—for many historical reasons—they represent the majority of people with access needs.

Again, generally speaking, visitors who develop access needs later in life often develop needs through aging, illnesses, or accidents that can change their lives. This group of people is also less likely to consider themselves as having access needs—why would they; they've gotten through life pretty well so far. They may also be afraid of asking for help because of their upbringing, or they may not know what is available to support them.

For this reason, these are perhaps the hardest people with access needs to show how they can still go on holiday, enjoy the arts, and learn.

For example, in my research I've discovered older people who visit museums or theaters after losing sight or hearing often shun mainstream access services.[3] These visitors will most likely approach the main desk, be helped by their families or friends who can see or hear better, and only want support—such as audio or written tour guides—that doesn't make them stand out from everyone else.

People who acquire learning difficulties later in life, such as short-term memory loss, will also still want to visit museums with others they've known most or all their lives. Similarly, these visitors will want to remember items they saw many years ago to help them feel comforted.

The third issue to address when developing access in cultural places is that the individual upbringing of any person, whether they have an access need or not, means visitors will all have very different social needs. And what's more, all these different needs will most likely rely more on visitors' early education, their family, and the people they've mixed with all their lives rather than their sensory problems or learning difficulties.

About twenty years ago, access was a simple matter of providing everyone with the same experience. Nowadays, however, access is smarter and we can provide people with a more bespoke experience if they want it—this can be referred to as a *visitor-led experience*. Alternatively, we can include people with access needs in regular classes, talks, and performances with visitors and audiences who have no access needs.

However, before beginning a vacation or day trip, you need to decide what kind of service you want, make contact with the cultural place you are visiting, and make it clear to them the type of access services you'll need. Similarly, the cultural place has to be prepared to listen to the individual access needs of its visitors or audiences.

What now follows are chapters on three different access needs—hearing, sight, and learning and memory—and the use of mobile technologies to access cultural places. Some people may have two of these access needs, others all three. However, whatever the situation, there should be a support strategy or a mobile technology function that can fit each specific need.

Chapter Two

Hearing Loss

It's difficult to know the exact number of people with a serious hearing loss in the US, as we don't know the extent of individual hearing losses and the effect this has on the people who have it. This is because many people with hearing loss don't go to see their doctors and don't think it's a serious problem or simply don't know what their hearing problem is. Others may not have access to proper testing for hearing loss.

If you consider the issue, this is largely a question of education, as we're so rarely told what good or bad hearing is, and we think it has to be far more serious before we get it seen to. There are also gaps in the way that we count people with hearing loss, as the range of loss can differ widely, especially when it's not reported.

In the US, the government's National Institute on Deafness and Other Communication Disorders, NIDCD,[1] is perhaps the main authority on the national picture of deafness. The last statistics the NIDCD published estimates around thirty-five million people have some form of hearing loss. This is over 11 percent of the population.

This said, as I write this chapter these estimates are old and based on statistics that have been out of date for ten years or more. It's actually likely that this number is now higher, as NIDCD also estimates there will be more than forty million people with hearing loss in 2025, meaning the number is growing—notably, NIDCD also predicts there will be over fifty million Americans with hearing loss by 2050.

Yet, hearing loss isn't just a problem for older people—although older people make up the greater majority of people with this loss. NIDCD also estimates that around 10 percent of all school-age children in the US have some form of hearing loss, and this loss could have a serious effect on their education and later life.

Despite this growth in numbers and awareness, NIDCD also estimates that less than one in three Americans with hearing loss use hearing aids. It's unknown whether this reluctance to wear hearing aids is because people feel embarrassed about wearing them, or they feel they can get by without them or, of course, there are people with no hearing at all for whom hearing aids would not work. In addition, hearing aids can be costly, and many do not work as well or for as long as their price tag might indicate. Access to hearing care and the affordability of treating hearing loss can vary widely. For instance, when I was writing this chapter my editor at Rowman & Littlefield told me her dad's hearing aid cost around $5,000 and still didn't work right.

All these statistics are worrying, as it means so many Americans are losing out on certain aspects of life by recognizing and adjusting for hearing loss.

There are various types of hearing loss, and as I wrote in the last chapter, each has its own separate frustrations. Hearing loss can bother and separate you from your surroundings, as we more often rely on speech for information and bonding. Though, this said, hearing loss shouldn't be pigeonholed, as many people won't share the same experience or need the same support because of this issue.

It's this support I turn to first in this chapter.

LIVING WITH HEARING LOSS

Generally speaking, we can think of hearing loss as being one of three types: complete hearing loss, partial hearing loss with tinnitus (the tone you hear in your mind to make up for the sounds you're missing), or partial hearing loss without tinnitus. Apart from the first type of hearing loss, this isn't about *how much* hearing loss you have, as many people have different hearing loss at different times; it's the quality of sound that's important.

One issue that many professionals have with hearing loss is thinking of it simply as a difficulty or an inability to hear or communicate. As I wrote earlier, this is only a part of sensory loss, both hearing and vision.

For many, hearing loss is a serious, personal, and social issue at work and during leisure times, and it can affect the enjoyment of a show, tour, or exhibition. It can also cause frustration and mean having to rely on alternative information, announcements, or technologies for something as simple as tickets or directions. At its most serious, this inability to communicate, work, and socialize can also cause stress or depression.

Without getting into numbers, total hearing loss is rare and visitors to tourist spots who have such a loss are more likely to use sign language. This said, people whom I've known to lose all their hearing in older age can be reluctant or find it hard to learn this new language, so they rely on written communications.

The more frequent types of hearing loss are the two types of partial hearing loss. And although these will have different effects, in terms of access these forms of partial hearing require similar support.

As with other access needs, writers often tend to talk about hearing loss as an extreme issue, assuming people either have hearing or they don't at all. Yet, there are many more aspects to hearing loss that make it hard to pigeon-hole individual types of loss, or to assume people providing support know what's best for any individual.

Hearing loss is personal to me. I grew up in a family with it and, as an adult, I've gotten used to my own hearing loss. In a way, this loss has become its own journey of self-discovery and reflection.

A FAMILY EXPERIENCE OF HEARING LOSS

My earliest experience of hearing loss is perhaps common to many readers and that of their families, with an experience of hearing loss and its related issues hitting older adulthood.

This isn't to say that these are the only experiences of hearing loss. *Although the greater majority of people with hearing loss lose their hearing in later life, there are also many experiences of early and congenital hearing loss, where the experience of culture is very different.*[2] However, my experience was of a particular type of hearing issues that passed through my family.

To begin with, for as long as I could remember my grandmother, Gran, had a heavy hearing loss. She was in her early seventies when I was born—I was the youngest son of the youngest daughter of the family, and I was her last grandchild—and for as long as I can remember, I had to be careful how I spoke to her. It wasn't just the words I said to her, it was the *way* I spoke to her.

There were also some other disturbances caused by her hearing loss that provided separate frustrations for Gran that we needed to consider every time we spoke to her. Gran had a sense of humor about these habits, but they were embarrassing for her. For instance, I remember the way Gran tilted her head when she listened to us and cupped one hand over an ear when she tried to hear. She would also look at me most intently when I spoke to her.

Something I didn't think of at the time but I now realize in hindsight was related to her hearing loss was the way that Gran wanted us to be quiet when we visited her. She was very old fashioned, with a traditional late-1800s upbringing. So when we paid our weekly visit to her house, my brothers and I often sat on the sofa and only spoke when we were spoken to.

We thought Gran's strictness was normal for someone her age, but now that I have a similar problem, I think she was strict because she needed to filter out frustrating background noises—practically, it was important to her that we only spoke one at a time.

Another thing I remember from my earliest childhood is that Gran became frustrated easily. She also became tired, and she couldn't handle us visiting for too long before becoming frustrated, something we often associated with an older person's crotchety behavior—my later studies show this lack of precise hearing commonly causes frustrations, something that must be considered when traveling or working with people with sensory loss.[3]

There were other physical issues connected to Gran's hearing loss that sometimes complicated her life more than she admitted. These other health issues can't be ignored when supporting general hearing loss.

I remember asking my mom about Gran's childhood. She told me Gran had frequent fainting spells. This was something we didn't associate with her hearing loss until later.

Gran also had problems balancing, something we felt was caused by an issue with her inner ear. She would never admit to her hearing loss or inner ear problems though, never visited a doctor or hearing specialist, and certainly never wore a hearing aid.

When I was an older child, I remember Gran's hearing loss became much stronger, and her hearing problems almost made the world around her unhearable. As this was happening, my eldest uncle got his first hearing aid, the first person I remember in the family having one, and importantly he admitted to this loss.

I remember feeling that it was strange my uncle had a hearing aid. He was a former soldier, extremely fit—even in older age—and enjoyed walking everywhere. He was also slim and distinguished, not someone I associated with a deafness that at that time people thought was a "problem."

Ironically, my uncle's hearing loss gave us a glimpse into Gran's hearing loss, and his openness and willingness to talk about his loss helped the rest of us later. More importantly, my uncle's description of his tinnitus helped me understand what Gran had gone through and what I'd experience later. He was a wonderful role model throughout my life.

The greatest role model I had to help me understand hearing loss, though, was my mom.

Among my earliest experiences of childhood were my mom's balance problems and fainting spells, which happened before she noticed losing her hearing. She'd had these problems as a child, she told me, but the most dramatic of these was her falling down our staircase in front of my middle brother and me at home. I was about four, and my brother about six.

As she lay in the well of our staircase, my mom calmly told us that she was going to pass out and that we shouldn't worry. I didn't know how to take this, and my brother and I were worried this was the last time we'd ever see her. It wasn't, and she came back to consciousness with me mopping her brow with a dampened flannel, as I'd seen people doing in the movies when a person was sick.

When I was a teenager, my mom got her first hearing aids, caused by a deafening tinnitus that came on the more stressed she was. We spoke about this, and her deafness was my first recognition that my mom, too, could lose her hearing like anyone else and had to adapt to a new situation. We tend to think of ourselves as safe in our bodies when we are this young, and only our grandparents and older relatives have these issues.

After this teenage experience, things changed. My mom got frustrated with conversations often, and sometimes it was frustrating to talk to her. As with Gran, it wasn't frustrating in *what* was said between us, as despite the usual family squabbles we became closer. It was the frustration of a naïve teenager, and then as a young and now older man wanting to speak to his mom as freely as he used to but being increasingly unable to do so.

One big lesson came from this experience: communication, as much as fondness, is a cornerstone of families. Not being able to talk as you once did is almost like not being able to kiss your mom or dad's cheek in the same way you once did.

Nowadays, it's a highly technical experience talking to Mum sometimes, as much on my part as it is on hers. We have to face each other as we talk, we have to talk slower and more clearly, and my mom has to be on "the right" telephone to hear me when we are both at home.

Public telephone conversations on my cell, something I try to do as little as possible, as it now also frustrates me, are nigh on impossible nowadays. And if I'm on a bus or in a train carriage, we get so loud with each other that people at the far end often become acquainted about our families' health, who's arguing with who lately, and what my children would like for birthdays and Christmas.

This form of talking also affects the emotion that we can put into our voices. One thing you may notice talking to people born with early and profound hearing loss is their voices have a different quality, and you need to remember the emotion is still there but in a different form.

It is, above anything, these seemingly small yet significant things that change your life as a person with hearing loss.

MY HEARING LOSS

I've written about the problems of functioning as a teacher in my previous book, *Cultural Heritage, Ageing, Disability, and Identity* and my essay "When Gucci Make Hearing Aids I'll Be Deaf."[4] But I think it's a good idea to go over the practicalities of this hearing loss again in more general situations.

I started noticing hearing loss and tinnitus in my twenties—even though before my twenties I was told off by my boss during a laboring job for not being able to hear him, although I'll never know whether this was his problem or mine. It wasn't a big issue at first, but it was certainly something I needed to check and keep on top of in my studies and my later jobs.

I managed to muddle through for years when I first noticed my hearing loss, as I had desk jobs and studies in my twenties that largely relied on written communications. However, it became more of an issue when I observed groups of people for long periods through my postgrad studies, and it became a real problem when I started teaching.

This, then, was my first big lesson in hearing loss: This loss isn't the same in all situations I encounter, and sometimes it's not a problem at all. It's only an issue when information is passed on and important to me, or when I have to concentrate on it and the spoken information has an effect on something I do.

My own hearing problem, much like my mom and uncle's problem, is worsened by tinnitus. At first, the tinnitus was not persistent, although occasionally strong, but then it became a permanent feature of my life. Also in common with my family, when I was a younger adult—unlike Gran, who had it as a child—I had fainting spells, sometimes passing out for short periods.

Occasionally, the fainting spells could give people the wrong impression about me. For instance, when I was lodging in a house in Toronto I remember coming to from a fainting spell and my landlady thinking I had drunk too much as my voice slurred just after I came to. It was certainly a shock for her and, even though she was a kindly person, it took some convincing that I wasn't drunk.

These fainting spells could also be physically dangerous. For instance, when I was staying in Tuscany, Italy, for a research meeting I once fainted in a bathroom in the middle of the night, cracking my head against the washbasin. Being Italy, all the surfaces in my bathroom were particularly tough ceramics and marble, and I fell hard and ended up with bruises and a lump on my head.

Also like my mom, uncle, and grandmother, conversation slowly but surely became a less spontaneous and more technical exercise. I found more than anything that I needed to see a person's face to hear him or her and I'd only pick up a certain amount of a conversation. Sometimes, I'd notice myself nodding along to what people were saying without understanding fully what they'd said.

Nowadays, when I have to listen to people for long periods, hearing loss has three main psychological effects on me: I feel frustrated and guilty by my inability to hear the person, it occasionally affects my balance if I have to stand for a long time, and it makes me very tired very quickly. The last of these issues is caused by having to concentrate on the person speaking, filter out background sounds, and interpret less information than people with full hearing.

The other thing I've noticed is my hatred of any background noise. In my teaching, it's important I get quiet in my classes and that I'm not in a situation with "tinkling" or "clattering" noises. These noises are the worst for my stress levels—the clatter of computer keyboards in class, if they are the old-fashioned type, can be off-putting and interferes with my general hearing. However, when I'm by myself and don't have to hear what anyone says, "tinkling" sounds can become my comfort blanket.

For more than one reason, but partly because of my hearing, I've also noticed I like my own company a great deal. This isn't only the frustration of not being able to hear a conversation all the time or finding it hard to joke as much as I did. It's also the tiring nature of having to concentrate on hearing.

Although I like my own company, I hate sitting in silent rooms and being by myself—which I realize seems a contradiction in terms. What I mean by this, though, is that I like the ambience of human chatter without knowing the people making it and without having to engage with the people making it.

This ambient noise is most important to people in general who have tinnitus, as for many this is the only time they don't hear the piercing sound constantly playing in their minds.

HEARING LOSS IN CULTURAL PLACES

There are four takeaway messages from my experience of hearing loss. First, hearing loss can be a genetic issue and, as such, you may have members of your family who are more sympathetic, patient, and supportive. Second, hearing loss isn't a total lack of hearing, and in fact noise can be good and bad. Third, the related psychological effects of hearing loss—such as tiredness, irritation, frustration, guilt, and stress—are often more significant than not being able to hear well. Fourth, hearing loss can often be part of a wider issue and can be affected by the inner ear, causing problems with balance. So anyone experiencing hearing loss should seek medical attention.

To support people with hearing loss, there are three main interventions that can help when you visit a cultural site: environment, technology, and information. These interventions often overlap.

Sign language users, signers, are perhaps the most straightforward to provide support for, and if you sign you are increasingly becoming known as a part of a different language group—a bit like a Spanish or French speaker.

This means that when you speak to someone using a different language—in this case, a spoken language—you'll need an interpreter.

This is, of course, an information intervention, although this can be a technological intervention where signers may be available via an app—although this is rare at the moment.

In many of the cultural places I've worked with over the years, signers can be hired if the site is given enough notice. This notice is vital as only but the biggest places, such as national museums, may have people who can interpret on site. Most cultural places, however, will have to hire freelance interpreters, usually from a specialist firm or agency.

In terms of their environment, as signing is almost entirely visual, signers need to stand or sit in clear sight of their sign interpreter, and the interaction is often two way. This is because signers sometimes need to clarify a word, phrase, or description, just as they do in spoken conversation. And as it can be seen as a different language, there are differences between signing and spoken conversation, including grammatical differences.

One exception to two-way signing is the signer in a theater or lecture hall who signs for a whole audience, in which case the signer will often stand just away from the main action.

Signing is also often done with the whole body, and it can be a physical performance in itself. As well as signing, a sign language interpreter will also mouth words, gesture through their faces, and use their entire body to express an idea or emotion. I've even seen signers shimmy like a dancer while explaining the story behind a picture.

As there is a need to use the whole body, signing for cultural places, especially theaters and museums, is best done standing up—although I've noticed sitting signers for lectures before. This means that signers will often need enough space to move and effectively sign their descriptions.

The lack of proximity to a sign translator can be particularly problematic, as regular tours with many people involve constant movement of the group. Similarly, theater performances are on a stage, higher than the audience, and in general distanced by the space between the stage and the theater seats.

Another issue with regular signing in theaters and some galleries is the lack of light or the variable light in theater performances, which makes signs more difficult to read. This is an intractable problem that theaters, monuments, and museums need to work on, but it can be minimized with careful planning.

One issue that many people don't realize about signing is that it often has a regional "accent" or gesture. This accent means that the relationship between signers and their interpreters is particularly important and can cause issues, such as misunderstandings about the features of artworks when signers are changed.

For instance, in a museum project I worked on recently we received complaints from a group of signers when their usual signer was not available one week. The complaint was caused when the alternate signer provided by the museum came from a different area where the group told me they had a different "signer's accent." This made most of the group feel uncomfortable about the nuances of the exhibition they were looking forward to.

For those people who don't sign, the environment is much more important, as is the use of amplification technology to enhance information.

Perhaps the biggest consideration is the acoustics in the environment. If you have low hearing, having even a slight echo or a sharp sound will mean the difference between hearing a tour or performance and not hearing it. Having *clean*, unfettered, chatter-free backgrounds can seem like aural champagne to a person with hearing loss.

This issue is perhaps where theaters have the biggest advantage and museums and galleries have the biggest disadvantage for people with hearing loss—particularly older traditional museums with classical walls and columns. So, when you're listening to a performance, tour, or lecture, although this will be the main sound in your environment, there may also be background, less important sound *pollution*.

As theaters are often designed and built with performance and ultimate representations of sound in mind, perhaps more than any other type of building, their acoustics are designed with care. For museums, however, the emphasis is on lighting the items they are exhibiting, often with little thought as to what can be heard in the environment.

Although everyone's individual hearing impairment has unique issues in each environment, there are elements of the environment that can make things easier for most people with hearing loss.

Generally speaking, the harder the surface the more it will reflect polluting sounds rather than absorb them, making hearing more difficult. This means glass, marble, tiled floors, and so forth cause more reflected sound—including the main performance itself—and more aural pollution.

Conversely, softer materials in the environment, such as wood, cloth, carpets, and natural environments—including the outdoors if there is no background noise—will help absorb extraneous noises. This means that noise pollution will be reduced and the frequencies of the performance will sound clearer.

As with signers, there are also visual considerations in the environment for people with low hearing.

For example, it helps if you have clear sight of a speaker's face when he or she is giving information in a cultural place. This is easier when the person talking is at an information desk, behind a counter or ticket booth, giving a personal guided tour, and so forth.

The science behind this is quite simple: hearing happens in the mind not the ear and is the product of all the senses, not just the sound from hearing. Perhaps strangely, your mind hears more through what you see than what you hear—that is to say, even if you hear the mouth saying a word, your mind will believe the word it "sees" more than the one it hears, an experience called the Colavita Effect.[5]

In practice, the Colavita Effect means that people with low hearing need to see the person saying the word in order to *hear* it better in the mind. This means that people with hearing loss need to sit toward the front of the auditorium during a performance and be close to the presenter during a tour.

In my experience, this need is only imperfectly managed. The person with low hearing will never be able to see the face of a guide in a museum or an actor in a theater all the time. Similarly, lighting will always be variable, as it will be lit for the performance or the exhibit rather than to develop access. However, access can be increased by telling a cultural place you're coming, by planning your seats, and by letting a guide know where you are.

The final consideration is the technologies, low and high tech, that are available for people with hearing loss. Commonly used technologies include captioning (where the description of what is being said runs along the bottom of a screen) and enhanced audio (such as loop systems and regular guides with headphones). Captioning can be made available through a cell phone or tablet, whereas enhanced audio systems have to be installed by the cultural place. People with mild hearing loss can also benefit from headphones that block out external sound and help people focus on the descriptions of artworks or the dialogue of a show.

The legal right to an accessible environment and to accessible technologies is stated by the Americans with Disabilities Act, which provides guidelines for cultural places. Practically, access to the environment for people with partial hearing loss is more of an issue than it is for people who sign. This raises important considerations for cultural places, including museums, theaters, movie theaters, galleries, sports stadia, and monuments—although religious buildings aren't included in the ADA.[6]

According to these ADA guidelines, if listening is at least a part of a visit to a cultural place, then the place needs to provide some form of accessible amplification. An obvious example of this need is in a theater, where plays, musicals, or movies will have dialogue or a soundtrack.

Museums, galleries, and monuments, however, are a little trickier to keep in line with ADA guidelines. As the ADA guidelines state, "In each assembly area where audible communication is integral to the use of the space, an assistive listening system shall be provided."[7] What these guidelines mean in practice is that if museums, galleries, and monuments provide a performance as part of their main service, they'll also need to provide assisted listening devices. For example, if a museum gives a regular guided tour or lecture, then they should also provide amplification or assisted listening through a device like an induction loop. The key word is *integral*: if the tour is part of a place's normal offering, they must provide a technology.

Importantly, the 2010 ADA guidelines also state that at least 25 percent of all assistive listening devices—which is a minimum of two devices if there are less than eight—need to be compatible with hearing aids. For cultural places, this means that planning technology with the design of an environment needs to happen hand in hand.

Chapter Three

Sight Loss

Mild sight loss is common. Think of the people around you who need glasses for reading or driving, particularly the number of people in middle or old age—in old age, this will likely be most people you know.

But of course, mild sight problems are not an issue for many. You can still read, still write—I've got my reading glasses on as I write this chapter—and of course see pictures, shows, or decorative objects, even intricate ones.

Visual impairments that are more severe make a huge difference to your life. This is serious sight loss that makes you unable to drive cars or do everyday tasks without help, not just sight loss that means you have to wear regular glasses on a daily basis.

If you're born with or develop serious sight loss, your whole life changes and your ability to access the arts becomes more difficult. As people who lose their sight in later life know, this sight loss is often accompanied by problems with well-being, as those with low vision may find it an emotional struggle to adjust. For instance, as Scott C. LaBarre wrote in a recent article for the National Federation of the Blind,

> For me, the emotions tied to this journey [of becoming blind] relate back to that day when I realized that I was blind and I would be so the rest of my life. Then, I felt trapped, imprisoned by the inability to see, and the inability to read and access knowledge. Fortunately, I have since realized liberation and freedom, and know that I can live the life I want. [1]

As LaBarre shows, people who lose their sight find it hard to adapt to a new form of reading and enjoying art. They find they need equipment to enlarge pictures, book texts, or newspapers, or in extreme cases they have to learn to touch-read Braille or 3D pictures.

This is a whole new realm of reading and understanding, and it requires a whole different skill set. You have to rely on other senses and language to appreciate pictures, shows, or objects.

And yet, despite these access needs we often *know* so little about sight loss or have any idea about its effects until we lose our own sight. What's more, although not as common as hearing loss, the latest statistics on the scope of sight loss reveal the true extent of this issue, making it puzzling why so little is done to address it.

For instance, a paper published in the medical journal *JAMA Ophthalmology* in 2016 estimated more than 4,300,000 Americans had some form of serious sight loss.[2] Interestingly, the same paper also estimated that more than eight million Americans had some form of untreated sight loss—although they didn't specify how serious this was.

What's more, the authors of the paper felt serious sight loss will grow significantly, with it estimated that almost nine million Americans will have serious sight loss by 2050.[3] By 2050, it's also estimated that more than sixteen million Americans will have untreated sight loss.

This serious growth will affect all communities, black and white, northern and southern, and men and women equally. This equal growth is largely because of an increasing average age of the national population reflected in those with sight loss developed in old age.

That said, although the average age of people with sight loss is rising, there is also a large number of young people with sight loss whose particular social and cultural needs need to be addressed.

For instance, my earlier research showed younger people with sight loss are less likely to visit museums or watch shows at any point in their life than people who lose their sight later in life. This reluctance is largely because it's assumed people with little or no experience of seeing won't be able to experience what are thought to be the visual arts or similar two-dimensional images.[4]

So, as with hearing loss, sight loss presents numerous issues in cultural places according to the background of the person and the type of sight problems he or she has. To support sight loss, we need to understand the nature of its different forms and the social and cultural experiences of people with sight loss, both past and present.

In this chapter, I look at these issues and examine solutions that can help people with vision loss in cultural places. This is not an exhaustive list but a look at ways in which you can get greater access in museums, theaters, and other cultural places to help you feel part of an exhibition or performance. I start this reporting by looking at different forms of sight loss.

TYPES OF SIGHT LOSS

Sight loss that affects people's lives can be caused by a number of overlapping causes and can be present in different ways.[5] The same is true of sight loss when you're accessing cultural places.

However, although there's a plethora of causes of sight loss, from genetics to accidents to disease, my previous work found that sight loss could usually be understood as one of three common types.

The first type of sight loss is what I call obstructive sight loss, such as floaters or cataracts. This type of sight loss either affects your peripheral vision (the outer limits of your sight) or the center of your vision, either through large obstructions or small blotches. At its most extreme, this form of sight loss can cause narrow views of the outside world like looking through a pipe, looking through water or a cloud, or looking through dirty binoculars.

Obstructive sight loss will usually result in slow reading and a need to look at material at very close quarters. In cultural places, writing on paper, signs, or screens will usually be unreadable without a great deal of help, but seeing colors of paintings is still possible and mobility can be adapted by using specialized equipment.

The most common terms for this sight loss are as follows: *tunnel vision*, where a person sees only a small area in the center his or her vision, with no exterior vision; *peripheral vision*, where a person sees only the outer areas of a sheet of paper or an environment, with the inner area being either distorted or missing; *floaters*, in which the sight is impaired by small blobs of distorted color and depth; and finally, what can be described only as *warped vision*, in which the depth, color, and outline of objects or text are misshapen, a bit like a hall of mirrors.

The second type of sight loss is caused by the unfavorable effects from light or by a brain injury. The term for this used by my friend Professor John Ravenscroft from Edinburgh, who is an expert in the field, is Cerebral Visual Impairment (CVI).

CVI will often result in slow reading and a need to look at material at very close quarters. Writing on paper and screens will again mostly be difficult to read depending on the combination of issues you have, and in many cases, colors won't be legible.

With CVI, you may not have much of what is termed a field of vision. That is to say, if you hold a page with writing below your chin, you may not be able to read it, or if someone is standing to your left or right, you may not be able to see him or her. CVI may also make you less mobile and affect your sense of balance or your use of facilities and equipment in cultural places, including bathrooms, cafes, or shops.

There are two outcomes of CVI that illustrate this form of sight loss well.

The first example is photophobia, which means something close to "fear of light." With photophobia, you may find it difficult to be around any form of light for too long. In extreme cases, this may lead you to freeze or become immobile if you sit or stand underneath strong light.

For instance, when I was a teenager my father had photophobia caused by his brain tumor, and we couldn't leave the strip lighting on in our kitchen when he might be around—I did once, and we found him rooted to a stool, unable to get up.

People who are photophobic will almost always have to wear dark glasses that filter out all but minimal light on a regular basis, even indoors.

The second example is achromatism, which means something close to "without color," in which a person will have no color perception, only shades—although this issue can also be caused by a lack of rods and cones in the eye. This issue is a form of color blindness that many people have, where they can't distinguish between certain colors, such as red and green.

However, there is an interesting issue with this condition. Although achromatism means that you may have impaired vision under normal lighting conditions, you may have better vision in dimmed light than a person without this condition.[6]

The third form of sight loss is of course total blindness, in which a person has no perception of light at all. This is perhaps the one form of sight loss that means you don't have to just adjust to regular living, as you tend to do when you have impaired sight. As a *holistic access issue*, then, total blindness *will* change the way you interact with the world.

For example, after losing your sight, you'll likely read Braille, 3D pictures, and sculptures by touch at an art gallery since you can not stand at a distance to read or appreciate art. Closeness and proximity to artworks becomes so much more important.

As well as touch, people who lose their sight completely have to rely on the digital voice of technologies such as cell phones, tablets, and audio devices for recording lessons and playing literature. Although these tactics are essential for people who are totally blind, they may also be useful to help people with sight loss too.

So, how has my experience helped me understand sight loss?

EXPERIENCES OF PEOPLE WITH SIGHT LOSS

Whereas my experience of hearing loss is largely due to growing up in a family with hearing loss from a young age, sight loss and the arts has influenced my work as an adult.

I think, on reflection, my motivation for working on access and sight loss was at least in part because of my love of visual arts. What's more, it could also be in part because I've seen cultural places unable to grasp the needs of people with sight loss more than people with hearing loss.

Perhaps more than hearing, seeing is so central to our cultural lives during our waking hours that we take it for granted. It's like a sensory habit we do unconsciously when we get close to a painting, a sculpture, a movie, or a play—seeing feels as natural as breathing.

Seeing is so normal and instinctive for most of us in cultural places that we take almost no time in our day to think about our own eyesight or how or why we see—we just see. We're reliant on vision psychologically for so many of our activities.

However, as I wrote in the introduction to this section, I've found the different life experiences of people with sight loss make a big difference in how they interact with museums, theaters, galleries, and other cultural places.

My first experience of working with people with sight loss was in an art-making studio in 1993. I was doing the fieldwork for my master's degree and helping out wherever I could in return—making hot drinks; getting tools, paints, paper, and clay; and even walking dogs.

The people I worked with were mainly from an older generation and had different forms of sight loss. However, although there was such diversity in class, the thing I noticed first was that people who had early sight loss all sat with one another. What's more, this group of people with early sight loss were more reluctant or totally unwilling to try making some of the artworks.

By contrast, the people who lost their sight later in life often sat in groups with other people with hearing loss and other forms of access needs, such as people with lesser mobility. Furthermore, these people with late sight loss were not just more willing to try making these pieces of art, they were also more willing to attend art museums than they were before they lost their sight.

This observation was made in a time when we didn't quite understand—although even in those days there was an inkling—that *even* people who were born without sight could understand images we thought were solely visual.

This was still an era when psychologies and philosophies believed people who were wholly without sight could only understand three-dimensional objects, and only through touch. This was an era before the first case studies of painters such as Esref Armagan by my colleague and friend Professor John M. Kennedy from Toronto (plus my own case studies) showed people born without sight could teach themselves painting.[7]

In many of the following years, I also found subtle differences between people with sight loss that made me realize there wasn't a single, typical person with sight loss. For instance, my academic mentor and PhD supervisor John M. Hull, author of the classic autobiography on sight loss *Touching the Rock*,[8] did not conform to a stereotype.

John had differing forms of sight loss and associated illnesses as a young boy in his native Australia, and he had been separated from sighted peers during different spells in his childhood. However, he achieved great things academically and never attended special schools. Subsequently, the persona he developed as a young adult was that of a "regular guy."

However, after passing his degrees, marrying, teaching in various schools, having his children, and entering academia, John's sight deteriorated rapidly, and he ended up losing his sight completely.

The transition from sight, albeit imperfect, to losing all sight was chronicled by John in a series of taped diaries and later transcribed as *Touching the Rock*. In its pages, and like LaBarre, John not only talked about the sense of loss he felt at losing his sight. He also described feeling a sense of loss of being one person, without knowing what it was to be another—that is, knowing himself as the person he was moving toward being.

The transition that John felt caused feelings of helplessness and depression until, ironically, he crossed over to becoming a man with no sight. It was then that he moved forward to accept his new self and could mourn the person he had lost.

This change of person—not just changing the sensations you rely on such as touch and hearing, but also a complete change of identity—is not unusual. And people who lose their sight as they are brought up and educated feel this change of identity most acutely.

So, what are the best ways of gaining access to cultural places after you have sight loss?

ACCESS NEEDS AND SIGHT LOSS

My friend and colleague Elisabeth Axel, from the New York–based educational charity Art Beyond Sight, suggests we've passed through three eras of arts education for people with sight loss—both partial and total sight loss.

The first era, from the end of the eighteenth century until the middle of the twentieth century, was that of radical teachers. Against the fashions of their times, these teachers taught students with sight loss to draw, sculpt, and mold as a form of perceptual and emotional self-awareness. These teachers, such as Wilhelm Klein and Viktor Lowenfeld, developed educational techniques by observing students and questioning their own ways of working.

In this era, the prevailing thinking was that a student's physical ability to see reflected his or her ability to enjoy or appreciate visual culture—the more you could see, the "better" at art you could be.[9] This ability was focused in those days on the fine arts, but it was later applied to theater, film, and television. In their era, radical teachers were thought to be attempting the impossible—or, at least, the highly improbable—to teach an understanding of "beauty" through touch.

The second era according to Elisabeth occurred in the second half of the twentieth century. In this era, scientists went against the beliefs of previous eras and even their own peers to change the minds of art institutions, schools, colleges, and museums. These scientists, such as John Kennedy and Morton Heller, suggested that perspective and line drawings could be imagined and created without recourse to sight.

According to Elisabeth, scientists supposed visual concepts were found to be simple cognitive puzzles that could be solved by various sensory means. They showed that visual properties of objects may be nothing of the sort, but merely information that was interpreted in the brain by various sensory means.

In what was described as this second era, I also observed myself that several groups of people with sight loss emerged to promote their own talents and understanding.

The first group of fine artists I was aware of through my work was National Exhibits by Blind Artists, Inc., a collective of artists with sight loss from Philadelphia.

National Exhibits by Blind Artists, Inc., was founded in 1974 at what was called the Library for the Blind and Physically Handicapped, a branch of the Free Library of Philadelphia. The series of shows was the idea of a group of people with sight loss who were regulars at the library and had persuaded its administrators to host an exhibition of their artworks.

The Library for the Blind's director at the time, Michael Coyle, was persuaded to host their first show, which was organized for the summer of 1975. Visitor numbers to this exhibition were large and many of the pieces were sold, making the exhibition profitable for the artists. The purpose of its early art shows subsequently became to promote the artworks of the collective as well as to teach the public about what the artists were capable of.

Similarly, the theater group Theater Breaking Through Barriers was formed in 1979 as a professional, Off-Broadway theater company. Theater Breaking Through Barriers began by recording studio-based plays for blind audiences, and broadcast through the In Touch Networks. The company then held acting classes at the Jewish Guild for the Blind, New York, and followed this in 1981 with a live production of Neil Simon's *Barefoot in the Park*. This was the first production we know of in the US to deliberately employ a blind and sighted cast.

Following this live performance, the company recorded a further series of studio-based plays, distributing these recordings across the country through the Library of Congress and local libraries for the blind. This work was followed by further live shows, including commissioned pieces such as *Whataya Blind!* which toured nationally.

According to Elisabeth Axel, we are currently living in the third era of art education for people who are blind. What's more, we have a growing acceptance of what was once thought to be radical thinking as mainstream thinking.

Nowadays, it's not unusual to think that people with little or no sight can successfully take an art class; turn up to a museum; feel, hear about, and see an object; or take on a drawing class. Art Beyond Sight now provides drawing sets for visually impaired children who request them. These are found to make the drawing process more inclusive and capable of being mastered by all children.

Just as the art education of people with low or no vision has gone through a cultural shift, so has the place of the voice and touch to describe objects or performance—this form of description is mainly termed audio description but is also known as verbal imaging or verbal description. Unlike art education for people with low or no vision, however, this change to description has largely been technical and linguistic rather than offering a revolution of attitudes.

For instance, in the early twentieth century the first recorded examples of audio description were basic guided touch tours with stuffed animals in Sunderland, England, and New York. In the 1980s, audio description moved forward thanks in part to new technologies, and were recorded for regular and specially commissioned pieces in art galleries.

These recordings often used what we now think of as clunky audio tapes on crackly old Walkmans—although let's be honest, we didn't think so at the time. Yet, these tours were very infrequent, often not well publicized, and rarely known about outside a selected few invited visitors.

Nowadays, we have highly sophisticated and well-researched recorded or bespoke real-time descriptions of artworks, theater performances, and films. These descriptions are also increasingly publicized and well-resourced, and many regular television remote controls have buttons that bring audio description into the home.

However, audio description, seeing with low vision, and touch are on the brink of a further cultural revolution, a new fourth era. We are now taking the description out of the hands of the sighted person and handing it to the audiences it was designed to support.

Description, touch, and the presentation of artworks are now within the powers of people with sight loss. In doing so, touch and description are made part of the design of artwork and description is made into its own form of performative art.

For example, an exhibition in San Francisco in 2017 called *The Gravity, The Levity* illustrates this changing of verbal description well.

THE GRAVITY, THE LEVITY—FAYEN D'EVIE
AND GEORGINA KLEEGE

Georgina Kleege, the verbal imager for *The Gravity, The Levity*, is a professor of English literature at the University of California Berkeley. She is the daughter of fine artists and was raised around New York. As a child, she often visited the city's museums, and through her parents she brushed up against painters and sculptors throughout her childhood.

Kleege is now a well-known author of nonfiction, much of which biographs her social and cultural experience of being raised as a woman with sight loss.[10] From her experience of touch tours and verbal imaging, Kleege feels a number of these tours regiment the experience of being visually impaired in the museum: they are only planned on certain days, at certain times. They also tend to include only a preselected group of people with visual impairments who are on a museum database.

On these tours, Kleege finds she is treated differently from those without sight loss, even though she's a professor. As important, she finds she often has to call or write ahead to let the museums know she's coming, and her group attendance is often based on a tour being available when she is on vacation.[11]

It's rare that Kleege or other blind museum guests or theater-goers can be spontaneous in their visits or be given permission to touch or have audio description in a museum or theater when turning up unannounced. These rare exceptions of spontaneous visiting are only made possible by well-thought-through solutions, such as

- contemporary, light, and portable technologies that can play recorded audio descriptions of artworks through apps that intelligently locate your place in the museum;
- accessible displays that people can touch and communicate with, which can respond with new and intelligent information;
- tours led by trained guides, known as docents, who know how to differentiate between the needs of visitors;
- access to mainstream tours, where descriptions can be delivered in different ways for all visitors; or
- *participatory description*, where each visitor is encouraged to add to an overall understanding of an artwork from his or her own unique perspective through a conversation about it.

For Kleege, the all too common separation of people with sight loss takes away a large part of the pleasure of being an attendee at a museum or gallery. This feeling of separation also restricts the aesthetic choices that visitors want to exercise for themselves. It makes people believe they can only go to cultural places with lots of help.

So, what's the solution to making people more welcome?

Although there is no simple answer to this question, Kleege feels that one possible contribution could be people with sight loss taking control of and curating their own exhibitions.

In what can be seen as a new phase of audio describing and touching, not so long ago Kleege took co-ownership of an exhibition for all by developing a project in partnership with artist Fayen D'Evie (fayendevie.com/).

This project involved developing a representation of D'Evie's exhibition *The Gravity, The Levity* as a touch exhibition with the audio description by Kleege. This audio description was based on Kleege's experience of touching the artwork and a lifetime working with fine art.

This different representation of D'Evie's work was exhibited at the Kadist Art Foundation, San Francisco, in 2016, with Kleege providing her own prepared description of the piece. As part of this exhibition, Kleege invited visitors with and without sight loss to touch the pieces themselves, allowing them to become a part of the exhibition.

Through work by people with sight loss themselves, audio description and getting to touch pieces is evolving rapidly, with the development of research and creative activity. More importantly, these ways of accessing artworks and the theater allow audiences with sight loss to take part ownership of exhibitions and performances.

Consequently, audio description and touch has moved from being a presentation of largely specialized information to a participatory art form with multisensorial references. Through this art form, audio description has also become a way of discussing artworks and performances with audience members, those with sight loss and those without alike.

By discussing audio descriptions and touch on tours, people with and without sight loss catch a glimpse into one another's cultural experiences. In this respect, audio description is becoming less of a support act and more of a way to help people with sight loss understand what was too long denied them.

Chapter Four

Learning Difficulties and Memory Loss

Learning difficulties and memory loss are often related. Both people with learning difficulties and people with memory loss often find it difficult to remember or concentrate on information, skills, or concepts.

Learning difficulties and memory loss are also issues that all of us will have at many points in our lives. This leaves us with important points to consider not just in this chapter, but also in this whole book.

First, learning is fundamental to our understanding of the world. Think of understanding and learning not in a nebulous, intellectual way. Think of learning at the level of knowing you need to eat, go to the bathroom, and walk, even knowing there is a world around us—perhaps our first act of learning.

Learning is our senses, as we learn to see, hear, smell, taste, and touch. Learning allows us to reason with our world. More about that later in the chapter. It is also the way we make sense of our cultural world; it is the way we know how to appreciate the information our community provides.

When we talk about learning difficulties and memory loss, then, we should never talk about a lack of learning or a lack of memory—you rarely actually lose memories and you never "not think." All of us remember and learn—this may be different to vision and hearing loss, where we literally lose our hearing or vision, but we very rarely lose what we have learned of hearing or vision.

So, having learning difficulties or memory loss just means that we find certain types of learning harder than others, the connections between our memories get damaged or distorted, or the neurons holding the patterns of our memories are damaged.

We may also find it difficult to concentrate or pay attention. Or perhaps we cannot concentrate on a single task or a type of learning too much. We may also find it difficult to remember certain types of facts or knowledge in our consciousness, our consciousness becomes disconnected from our sub-consciousness, or our subconscious cannot process the signs and symbols of our emotional connections easily.

Second, everyone is on a *spectrum* of memory loss or learning difficulty—this is often the term used by educationalists, and it is best imagined as a chart going from little memory loss to greater memory loss. Many of us will spend our lives close to the bottom of this spectrum, needing only minimal support at most points in our lives.[1]

However, when learning difficulties and memory loss move further up the spectrum, this issue becomes serious and obviously more specialist support is needed. For many of us, we will experience these difficulties as a supporter or caregiver. We may have to support an elderly relative, spouse, or partner as they move up into what I call the *support zone*.

Subsequently, like hearing and vision loss, learning difficulties and memory loss are complicated issues. However, unlike sight and hearing loss, they have unique challenges when visiting cultural places and planning travel.

To begin with, if your main issue is a difficulty in specific types of learning, you usually acquire this difficulty as a young person or you are born with it. Unlike visual and hearing issues or memory loss, you may not discover this issue until later in childhood, when you start to enter education. This means you may not know you have an issue until you find visiting places hard, and this can put you off making visits afterward.

For example, if you are high on the dyslexia spectrum, you usually discover this issue when you first learn to write, which is usually your early school years. Similarly, if you find it hard to concentrate on a single task for a long time, those around you may only discover this when you first start school or kindergarten.

The support we provide for people with many learning difficulties or memory loss is often a combination of three different types of support in differing degrees and qualities: learning, information, and emotional. It's the last of these three that's the hardest to provide and is often misunderstood.

For example, I've worked with students who find it difficult to concentrate. Quite often, these students feel guilty or stupid because others can concentrate longer while they often lose interest in what they're learning. This often leads to something considered naughty, such as scribbling on walls or desks. These students are then considered to have a general behavioral problem. They either will be given lesser learning tasks (often way below their ability) or they will get sent out of class or banned from class trips or activities. Instead, they need a specialized response to their learning difficulty, not a punishment for bad behavior.

The rest of this chapter delves into the issues surrounding learning difficulties and memory loss in greater detail. I then write about specific examples of how people with learning difficulties can be supported in cultural places.

To begin this process, I start with the fundamental issue of how we learn to learn as we age, and the place of our memory in this process. For without understanding how we learn and remember, we won't fully understand learning difficulties and memory loss or the people who need support in these areas.

THE NATURE OF LEARNING, MEMORY, AND AGING

There is disagreement among psychologists, philosophers, and educationalists alike about what and how we learn and when. There is also a fierce debate about what is learned naturally and what we learn through being socialized.[2]

There is general agreement among those who study learning, however, that we are all born with a capacity for some form of learning. What's more, there is a general agreement that we end life knowing more than when we entered it.

The philosopher John Locke wrote in the later years of the seventeenth century that we are all born as a "Tabula Rasa," a blank slate. It is on this slate that the story of our lives is written through learning, and all our learning is developed through experience.[3]

As I wrote earlier, we now know that we're all born without sight, hearing, and knowledge.[4] We learn and develop our senses and what we know and remember—both being two sides of the same coin—as we grow up.

As we age, our memory also changes. The way our brain searches for, processes, creates relationships between, and retrieves information and sensory memories changes. This change or "loss" of our previous memories leads to natural difficulties in learning and the way we engage with our environment—there is no such thing as memory loss, it's just harder to get at or the connections between memories becomes broken.

However, despite the dependence of memory on learning and learning on memory, for practical purposes learning and memory are often observed in different ways.

For those of us over fifty, it's quite natural that we start to forget more and more as we age. We put keys in the wrong place. Or we put keys in the right place and then forget where the right place is.

I often find it difficult to remember the names of people or important jobs I have to do at work nowadays. So, I now write down as much as I can in a list, because if I don't I'm not confident that my daily tasks will get done.

As we age, our thinking will also slow and our responses and reflexes won't be like they were when we were young. Although, of course, this doesn't mean we will have significant problems in old age or that many of us won't still be productive and hardworking citizens.

As a father of two young children, Nick and Fia, I'm constantly amazed how much they remember of the most banal details they find in magazines or on television: cartoon characters' names and superpowers, sport stars' names and teams, where all these people are born, where they were in their childhood, and even their families. Frustratingly, they also remember promises I make in the hope that they'll forget them.

I'm also constantly amazed at how quickly Nick and Fia are learning to turn and move as they run and play, how adept they become with bat and ball. Although at three, Fia needs more help than Nick, whose body is more developed.

At eight, Nick is not as strong as I am yet and won't overtake my strength for perhaps another ten or fifteen years—I hope. He has to reach maturity of course, and his sensory-motor skills still need time to ripen. But I know already how difficult it is to catch him when he's running with his ball and how difficult it is to keep up with his stamina for more than the shortest bursts of energy.

The philosopher Piaget wrote about children's physical and mental progress in the mid-twentieth century, based on his own observations of his children. Importantly, he wrote about approximate stages of child development at different ages.[5]

Substantial parts of Piaget's theories are admittedly criticized now as being a little naïve, as he was too rigid in describing these stages and the ages at which they occurred. But it is generally held that children do progress in different ways at different times. This fundamental principle still holds true.

What Piaget failed to notice, however, was the continued changes in the learning patterns and memorization of adults. In a learning and memory sense, it could be said that childhood never ends.

As I age, memory becomes a strange beast I must control. I remember things I learned when I was a teenager or in my early twenties: I remember what deoxyribonucleic acid (DNA) is and how to spell it; I remember the chemical formula for glucose created by photosynthesis for some reason ($C_6H_{12}O_6$); and, like my children, I remember banal intellectual details, like the Russian psychologist Lev Vygotsky's middle name (Semenovich, by the way).

However, as I age, I can't remember things I did ten minutes ago, or things I have just done. It means I must ask my wife if I have just taken my vitamins each morning. I often have the bottle on the breakfast table but can't quite remember if I've swallowed them yet. If my wife isn't around, I look at the level on my glass of water as a reference point.

As I've aged, learning has also become easier, in a way. My understanding of concepts has sharpened and become more sophisticated. Communication of ideas has also become better—the fact I'm writing this, my seventh book, is a miracle given my earlier struggles with literacy as a young man.

I'm also differently confident about my writing, *laissez-faire* sometimes, and have a settled writing style honed over twenty-five years. These are regular learning issues that shape and color my adult life and help me develop further as an older adult.

Even though my learning prowess has not yet weakened, I tire more easily when I concentrate for long periods. I find writing all-nighters almost impossible nowadays. And the older I get as learning issues start to creep in, the more I'll need support. With luck, however, these will never become too serious.

This concept is very different from my children, who still need to develop their minds and have yet to identify and work on any regular "blind spots" in their learning capabilities—although Nick approaches math puzzles with ease already.

Nick, Fia, and I can overcome our issues at the moment through simple strategies we can learn ourselves, or I can teach Nick and Fia in the course of parenting.

I often find myself hoping they will remain on this upward curve of absorbing the world's wonders, their environment, and the people and communities they belong to. Hopefully, the learning difficulties they experience are regular and do not require support.

They should learn about the world around them with only safe amounts of stress. They should also learn to learn as my wife and I did by passing through phases where what we learned became less painful. I hope they won't suffer the humiliations that some students I taught felt when they found this process difficult—this is perhaps the hardest part of being a teacher and seeing your students lose their sense of self-belief.

So, given this understanding of lower-on-the-spectrum learning difficulties and memory loss, what happens when these learning difficulties or memory losses move up the scale? For practical purposes, I will treat people with learning difficulties and people with memory loss separately. As I wrote earlier, the former are usually born with their learning difficulties, and the latter often acquire memory loss later in life.

WHAT HIGHER-ON-THE-SPECTRUM
LEARNING DIFFICULTIES ARE

First, it's important to define what is meant by a higher-on-the-spectrum learning difficulty, one that can lead to problems with memorization, and what it means to have a learning difficulty. According to the National Center for Learning Disabilities, Inc., serious learning and attention issues will affect one in five of us. These include

> brain-based difficulties in reading, writing, math, organization, focus, listening comprehension, social skills, motor skills or a combination of these. Learning and attention issues are not the result of low intelligence, poor vision or hearing, or lack of access to quality instruction.[6]

Although this is a good starting point, there are caveats that such a necessarily broad definition can't cover. Learning is, of course, far more pervasive than education—two concepts people often mistake for each other.

As I wrote earlier, learning is something we do all day, every day, no vacation, no break during sleep—yes, we even learn while we sleep. Learning can be helpful, but—and this is important to understand—learning can be harmful, and we can learn damaging habits and emotions. For instance, learning to suppress certain emotions such as sadness after a tragedy or serious incident can psychologically and physically harm us.

By contrast, education is a system of learning developed by our communities and countries. It makes us part of our culture and our culture part of us—be it the culture of our nation, our religion, or even our ancestors—and it is rooted in language, symbols, and allegory.

So, when we talk about serious learning difficulties further up the spectrum, we are typically talking about finding it difficult to do tasks that are part of our lives, not just part of our schooling. It is something that slows learning and makes concentration on a single problem or task difficult.

There are also cases where we mistakenly talk about educational difficulties when we talk about learning difficulties. However, to add to our confusion, many specific learning difficulties are also not related to medical conditions and are "diagnosed" by educational psychologists. For instance, issues such as dyslexia, dyspraxia, or dyscalculia are often identified initially by parents and teachers, and then diagnosed formally by educational psychologists.

Given early identification and support, specific learning difficulties usually have relatively mild consequences. They will not change a child's life in a significant way in comparison to many other life changes. However, these learning difficulties *will change the way* they travel through life.

As we move up through the spectrum of learning difficulties, these issues will become more serious. In these circumstances, support requires greater patience and skill, and the issues that require support can include medicalization.

For instance, perhaps one of the learning difficulties discussed most is what we usually call "Down syndrome"—it is usually written in several different ways, as it is named after the doctor who first described this issue.

Down syndrome is caused by a genetic mutation that provides an extra chromosome in a fetus. Despite sounding innocuous, this extra chromosome causes learning disabilities, physical and sensory impairments, and health issues. Children born with Down syndrome also often have a shorter height than other children.[7]

As cell mutation is more likely when you are older, the older parents are at the time of birth, the more likely it is that a baby will be born with an extra chromosome.

For example, if a mother is twenty years old at the time of birth, then the baby will have only a 1 in 1,500 chance of having an extra chromosome. However, if a mother is forty years old at the time of birth, then the baby will have a 1 in 100 chance—a 1 percent chance—of having the extra chromosome.[8]

To put this in context, even though this chance remains slight, mothers are fifteen times more likely to have a baby with an extra chromosome if they have a baby at forty rather than twenty.

Nowadays, babies with Down syndrome are usually identified during pregnancy and if not at birth. When children are born with Down syndrome, they most often have what is termed hypotonia, that is, a lack of physical strength. These babies will also have a lack of physical movement and are significantly smaller and lighter than most other children.

Slightly older babies with Down syndrome may also have related hearing or vision issues. Later in life, people with Down syndrome are also more likely to have health problems with their heart, lungs, or liver, although people with Down syndrome are now living longer than ever before.

HIGHER-ON-THE-SPECTRUM LEARNING DIFFICULTIES AND CULTURAL PLACES

Day-to-day understanding, self-awareness, and concentration by people with learning difficulties further up the spectrum are noticeably slower and harder. People further up the spectrum also find it increasingly difficult to remember information in books or sheets. They will almost always find reading complex words, longer sentences, or paragraphs more difficult.

So, cultural places first and foremost need to rethink the way they provide information and communication for people with higher-on-the-spectrum learning difficulties.

Learning difficulties higher on the spectrum also often make it harder for people to understand abstract concepts, such as historical periods or complex math. Teaching concepts to people higher on the spectrum can stress these learners and can lead to an avoidance of learning or episodes of upset—a bit like anyone if they are given problems that are too hard to handle.

Though learning and concentration can be difficult and stressful, in my experience many people with serious learning difficulties often find learning in cultural places more enjoyable. There are three reasons for this.

First, cultural places often provide what is called *concrete learning*, that is, learning mainly through the senses and learning about objects or concepts directly, step by step. For instance, if you want to teach a person who finds learning about electricity difficult, it is good to switch on a lightbulb and explain a current running through its visible wire. After this, people will generally find it easier to understand that electricity is a moving energy and can power other objects like motors.

Showing someone this process and then building on this knowledge slowly, rather than starting to teach people about electricity by showing them a circuit diagram, is called scaffolding—picture the way we learn like climbing a building scaffold bar by bar. This is a concept first described by the Russian psychologist Lev Vygotsky[9] (whose middle name I mentioned earlier in the chapter) and has been applied effectively by educators for decades.

This is where cultural places fit in well. Cultural places like science museums can show people the light bulb and describe the process as it demonstrates. They give you buttons to press, wheels to turn, buses and rockets to sit in, and even the smell of old engines.

Not only this, these museums can show you, literally, the evolution of the earliest engines to the newest engines with everything in between. This makes understanding how we have the machines and objects we have today more "real" to the viewer.

Attending theaters and cinemas works on the same principle. For instance, studying Shakespeare or Elizabethan England in class can be difficult. High school can rarely represent what the streets, dress, houses, and characters were like five hundred years ago, in Stratford-upon-Avon or London, England.

However, when you watch a play by Shakespeare, hear the language spoken as it was at the time, and are surrounded by a set designed in the round, the whole era comes to life. This is why historical films can be such dramatic illustrations of human lives. If you can suspend your disbelief, they can take you to these otherworldly places and eras, even for the briefest of moments.

The second reason people with learning difficulties often enjoy learning in cultural places is because cultural places don't assess visitors or insist you learn at a particular pace or keep up with the rest of the class.

For instance, in a recent museum project in Europe I found that people with learning difficulties learned about art by being part of groups that visited galleries every fortnight. During their visits, they were taught about different objects in the collections. They chose different paintings and their own descriptions. They were told about selected galleries and the difference between these galleries and others.

During the project, we worked out communication rules as a group, and we learned how exhibitions are put together and the decisions that are made about what is to be exhibited. Even those who had rarely or never attended museums began to learn how to visit these places and appreciate them.

What was most interesting about this experience was that the people who were higher on the spectrum often had learned little about the history of art before. At the beginning, they recognized few paintings and knew little about even the most famous artworks they saw. So, we asked the participants in this project to tour, interact with, and then describe these experiences in language they felt comfortable with. This form of description is also called "social stories" and is offered by many of the museums I write about later. Subsequently, we adapted the information we provided as *Easy Read* literature. [10]

At the end of the project, these participants could give you the names of artists and navigate their way around the largest and most complex national museum by the galleries. They were also sorry when the project finally finished and they would not have to attend every fortnight.

It is this sense of fulfilment that museums can provide. When learning doesn't come with strings attached, people are often drawn back in. These museums, theaters, and similar cultural places hold some of the most important representations of culture, preserved in time, so learning about these things in your own personal time is important.

Third, cultural places such as museums and theaters are an important part of our physical and psychological well-being. This is an important fact that is too often overlooked when planning a vacation.

People higher on the spectrum of learning difficulties are traditionally also more susceptible to obesity [11] and depression [12]—and depression can also cause learning and educational difficulties of its own. But visiting places, getting around town, and meeting with all kinds of different people as a form of exercise can make us happier, reduce our cholesterol, and reduce our chance of getting diabetes. [13]

Cultural places that encourage touch and interaction, such as science and children's museums, are also particularly good for the physical development of children with learning difficulties. This is largely because children higher on the spectrum are generally not encouraged to exercise as much as children lower on the spectrum are.

For example, children with certain forms of learning disabilities, such as Down syndrome, may have issues developing sensory-motor skills. These skills are the way we clutch, hold, or pick up objects; grip onto things we are climbing onto or up; and use our hand-eye coordination.

In this way, the greater opportunities children have to go to places where they can move their hands, hold and carry objects in exhibitions, grip and move handles and wheels, expose themselves to bright or changing and moving colors, and have different experiences of noise that they have to react to, the better.

MEMORY, AND WHAT HIGHER-ON-THE-SPECTRUM MEMORY LOSS IS

Memory is layered, and our memories of things, images, events, and people don't remain like snapshots in the brain that can be retrieved at will. Instead, our memories should be thought of as a process that is constantly in flux: our short-term memories being like flowing tidal waters and the long-term memories like the sand below. [14]

In its state of flux, short-term memories are manufactured in the mind. The "picture" of the world around us is then manufactured as moving images, sounds, smells, sensations, and tastes all working together. For want of a better phrase, these are called *sensory memories*.

These *sensory memories* are affected by language, which connects these new memories with existing long-term memories. In this way, short-term memories can be imagined as our working memory, whereas our long-term memory is a database of stored information that we need to learn, plan, and have exist.

For instance, if I see my friend Patrick on the street, my senses first compute that this is Patrick by focusing on his recognizable features, usually his face. The information that this is Patrick is retrieved from my long-term memory, and my working memory of my friend is a form of learning. Consequently, disruptions to this process also become a form of learning difficulty.

During my encounter of him, I learn to identify Patrick in a new way, most often by what he looks or sounds like. This is because, even though perhaps only slightly, Patrick is never the same person I've seen before.

For example, even if I saw Patrick the day before, he will most likely be wearing different clothes the day I now see him. I may see Patrick under different lighting conditions or with different background noise. If I see him a year later, particularly at our time of life, Patrick will look older than he did, but not enough that I don't recognize him.

However, my memory will not stop working there. This working memory during the day stays in flux and builds up until I can reach a relaxed state, which is most often after I've fallen asleep. During this period of relaxation, my short-term working memory developed during the day, including my memory of Patrick in the street, will move into my long-term memory—a process called *consolidation of memory.*

This process of moving short-term, working memory to long-term memory may be seen in my mind through dreams. During these dreams, these memories will wax and wane on my consciousness. During dreamtime, my emotions connected to Patrick from our conversation and the past will be associated with images and stored, and at this point symbols and allegories from my past may reappear.

Subsequently, like everyone else, my most resilient memories are my long-term memories. This is because these memories are not merely an episode, a single experience, or a once-learned skill. These are associations and bonds in our memory that are added to again and again and layered with associations and emotional litter.

Constantly reinforced long-term memories of tasks, spaces, and places also build very strong patterns in our memories. For instance, if I catch a bus and walk the same route to work day after day, the route is reinforced in my mind again and again. If I try to deviate from that route on a workday, this new experience may prove stressful; I become confused and nervous about trying this new route again. None of us like change, as it challenges these reliably set concrete long-term memories.

We still have a great deal to learn about memory, particularly the biological processes that happen when we develop memories and when we have memory loss. But we know that the memory contains this series of associations in the brain. When memories are formed efficiently, like the senses, these associations are manufactured inside the mind as electrical and chemical connections at a molecular or even atomic level.

In other ways, the most common types of higher-on-the-spectrum memory loss are related to damage of or chemical imbalances in certain parts of our brains. These issues may damage storage areas in the brain, confusing our memories or memory acquisition and storage. Otherwise, toxins or chemical imbalances can impair the retrieval, storage, or associations of memories.

In rare cases, brain errors are brought on by sudden events, such as accidents, drug overdoses, or strokes. More commonly, these events build and worsen over a period of time, caused by microscopic plaques in the brain or toxins changing the retrieval or use of memories.

More common causes of memory loss include taking narcotics regularly over a period, drinking too much on a regular basis, and being a regular cigarette or cigar smoker. Lack of sleep and of course our normal aging process are also commonly linked with memory loss: aging will decrease the generation of our brain and nerve cells, and a lack of sleep creates chemical imbalances and impediments to our body's detoxification process.

For example, one of the best-known forms of higher-on-the-spectrum memory loss is dementia, an issue that mostly affects older people. Despite assumptions about dementia, it has no single cause like a cold or the flu; instead, it is referred to as a syndrome, which is to say it is a collective pattern of symptoms. [15]

Common to all these symptoms is a progressively poor short-term memory, with older memories mistaken for present or recent experiences, objects, and people. What's more, people with dementia also often forget people who are part of their life, mistake names of people, and mistake people who are young for older or dead relatives.

Dementia's other symptoms can include problems concentrating, speaking, understanding recent topics in the outside world, knowing where you are, calculating, and problem-solving. There are also occasionally psychiatric and behavioral symptoms linked to dementia, with people hallucinating and becoming aggressive as a result of the stress of their confusion.

In the longer term, this leads to a change of personality and emotions, as well as depression. Like some forms of learning difficulty, dementia can also cause physical difficulties, such as issues with mobility, seeing, hearing, eating, and dressing. People with dementia also become increasingly frail and often lose weight and muscle tone.

HIGHER-ON-THE-SPECTRUM MEMORY LOSS
AND CULTURAL PLACES

Higher-on-the-spectrum memory loss is particularly difficult for the caregivers of people with dementia. Often their close relatives, spouses, or partners are older and frailer themselves. These supporters are also at risk of depression and other mental health issues, as they often remain isolated and under stress from seeing those they love disappear into a cloud of fear.

It is this physical and psychological well-being of people with higher-on-the-spectrum memory loss and their caregivers that cultural places are particularly good at supporting. [16] There are three areas of support, one of which is also good for caregivers as well as for relatives, spouses, or partners.

The first area is sensory stimulation. Attending plays or movies, moving between galleries, and experiencing artworks stimulates our senses. Having day trips and vacations in interactive environments, particularly sensory areas outdoors or where exhibits can be handled, also helps stimulate body movement and makes the muscles healthier.

The second area where cultural places can help is the comfort that people with dementia feel when surrounded by objects that they may recognize from the past—or see exhibits with a style of painting or sculpture they have seen before. As confusion over short-term memory means that modern objects and events can be confusing, experiencing artworks from decades or centuries ago can be familiar and reduce stress.

Imagine stepping out of a time machine where you are transported to a different time and, instead of an unfamiliar world, everything is as it should be. This is the world that people with higher-on-the-spectrum memory loss can feel on a daily basis in their everyday surroundings.

The third way that cultural places are good for both those with memory loss and caregivers is that they are a place to bond and exercise. Exercising in a calm environment is important for people with higher-on-the-spectrum memory loss. Importantly, they can move gently through a calming space, which doesn't put too much stress on the body but means people can still practice movements.

Bonding in cultural places is particularly good for caregivers, who can share their experiences of living with those people they care for with others who will understand what they are going through. Expressing these feelings can help reduce the risk of depression and develop networks they can call on later when things get worse.

Happily, many galleries and museums are beginning to understand how useful their spaces and services can be and are now providing special tours for people with higher-on-the-spectrum memory loss. For example, one of the earliest museums to offer tours for people with dementia in the US was the Museum of Modern Art (MoMA), New York, in the early years of the millennium—the tour was developed with the wonderfully titled group Artists for Alzheimer's.[17]

Famously, during these tours MoMA chooses times when there are few visitors or the museum is closed. Normally, including people with impairments or access needs only outside museum hours is frowned upon, but for people with dementia this is necessary, as it reduces stress for visitors. MoMA also makes sure to keep the number of visitors for their tours low—they allow only eight to ten people with dementia plus their caregivers or other family members.

For learning, MoMA is careful not to teach too much or challenge their visitors' memories too much, so the museum uses small amounts of simple knowledge. Subsequently, their tours contain only four to six artworks, each of which is based on an ever-changing theme. As they describe:

> We purposely selected works by artists of different backgrounds who worked at different times and were from various geographical regions. In addition, the works present an interesting overview of several key styles and techniques, while giving very different interpretations of the modern city. These points

offer intriguing opportunities for discussion and exploration, and allow participants to tap into their own lives and experiences.[18]

During each tour, time is allowed to move between artworks and galleries, as
visitors take in the instructions and information. In addition, they add in
numerous breaks, so the visitors have time to rest. MoMA also makes sure to
encourage regular visitors, have toilets and medical facilities at hand, and
have lighting and sound that is more ambient than normal, all of which
reduce visitor stress.

Chapter Five

Mobile Technologies and Cultural Places

Not many people think of their cell phones or tablets as being a way to access vacations or day trips. Yet, nowadays these technologies can be the best way of getting to and around cultural places, and to enjoy learning as you do so.

This chapter introduces ways your cell phones and tablets—what educators and cultural professionals call mobile technologies—and the apps they use have helped to transform the accessibility of our vacations. For practical reasons, in this chapter I focus on the accessible apps on Apple and Android (the latter is produced by Google) operating systems, which covers most devices—to add in all other mobile technologies would take many more chapters and change the feel of this book.

Whether you're using existing technologies within cultural places, specially designed apps, or customized settings on loaned or personal devices, you can benefit from these technologies.

Mobile technologies are particularly useful for visitors with access needs, as numerous professional supporters find they provide good technological support functions. What's more, their manufacturers claim that they are among the most accessible technologies on the market.

More important, these technologies are light and can be personalized, they are easy to use, and they allow you to interact with cultural places in ways that up until recently were never imaginable. These devices often have impressive computing power for their size, lightness, and price. They can easily play videos and sound files, search online databases, and even plot your routes on vacations or day trips.

My cell phone, for instance, has many functions that my desktop computer had five years ago. Come to think of it, my cell phone has nearly as many functions as the laptop I'm writing this chapter on now. More interestingly, it has several times more computing power, memory, and functions than the desktops I used as a teacher almost twenty-five years ago.

Consequently, this technology has changed the way we think of computing to support us, and it has changed the ways we can now interact with our surroundings and other people in cultural places.

The trouble with this rapid advance is that technology changes too quickly for professionals, cultural places, and visitors to keep up with the use of these machines—I personally struggle to know what is on the market at any one time. And so, only a few museums and theaters have really harnessed their true power and few visitors know how best to use their machines when they visit.

This chapter looks at the different ways you can best use your technologies on vacation. It also provides tips for working with this book to find information and communicate with cultural places.

USING TABLETS AND CELL PHONES
IN CULTURAL PLACES

Mobile technologies are softly revolutionizing the ways in which we provide support for people with access needs. They are being used to support all ages, with students from small children to college seniors using these devices for reading, researching, and even writing reports. They support people at work to communicate and store accessible information, whether in their pocket or their briefcase. They also allow older people who are isolated in their homes to communicate, share their thoughts, and see their children and grandchildren from afar—as my own mom does.

More importantly, these technologies are being used by people of all ages and access needs to communicate with one another, arrange transport, or even find accessible services, from local buses to public bathrooms.

I personally experienced using technologies to support people with access needs with a student, Emma, whom I supported in an engineering class shortly after I started teaching at the college level.[1] After seeing her learn to download books with her tablet and use its camera to zoom, I got bolder and developed a new college project to help more students with access needs who'd struggled in class.

During lunch sessions, I taught mobile technology study skills to students with access needs who found it difficult to attend regular classes. The students who attended were all volunteers and all had their own devices. They attended my sessions because they found it difficult to hear or see the teacher, read materials, organize themselves, carry heavy technologies, or access the whiteboard or papers they were given.

In a second project, colleagues and I also set up an online learning site where students could access information and, more importantly, share their own skills and tips. Embarrassingly, this website proved to be more popular than my sessions because it provided flexibility—students often couldn't get to lunch sessions—and because the students liked the anonymity of learning through the website.

The website stayed up for a while, and it was interesting for me to see students still adding to it months after my lunchtime sessions finished. There were real skills out there that students learned themselves that I wasn't aware of, and their anonymity allowed them to live in a parallel learning universe, one where they felt comfortable.

Following this second project, my colleagues and I published a paper that described how mobile technologies were used during this project and what the students got from them. In this paper, we wrote about three staple skills that college students seemed to need and that we could teach using tablets and cell phones: (1) making and sharing notes as written, audio, and video files; (2) sharing and organizing information through written, audio, and video files; and (3) taking pictures and recording audio and video files—either at the same time or separately.[2]

In the process of supporting students and developing these special projects, I also found Apple- and Android-based functions and apps were grouped in two different ways: the types of information we need to learn and communicate—that is to say, written, audio, photographed, or video formats—and the gestures needed to get at this information.[3]

These two functions, of course, went well beyond the skills college students needed. Importantly, they looked at all types of learning and numerous day-to-day activities that could be supported through mobile devices. For example, one of the functions we looked at was video calling, which helped people with hearing issues communicate with friends and family by seeing their face or using sign language.

A year or so after the first course, and getting back to arts inclusion, other colleagues and I developed short photography courses for cultural places using tablet computers and cell phones. These skills were designed around creating, managing, and swapping information in a number of different ways with other visitors at cultural places, whether they had access needs or not.[4]

These short courses were slightly different, though. Although my first project was designed to support people with access needs to work in regular classes by providing special lunchtime sessions, this left a paradox: I was teaching these students separately, which is what I had designed study skills to avoid. These new short courses taught people with serious access needs alongside those with minor or no access needs together, and they were designed to create the same or similar skills.

So, what lessons were learned from this process?

The first lesson to arise from working with mobile technologies was that human issues unrelated to access needs were paramount to their use: the engineering student needed to learn to read scientific materials, and her tablet allowed her to do this; the students preferred to learn and develop skills through an online platform than attend lunchtime sessions, as it provided a certain amount of anonymity; it is better to develop skills with tablets and cell phones through general sessions rather than having separate sessions for people with access needs.

The second lesson was that the devices didn't need to reveal the true identity of the users or their needs; this allowed people to keep their needs anonymous at college and in cultural places. In this way, it also helped them develop a comfortable way of seeing themselves: in need of support but not needing a supporter, a technological outsider but also a technical expert. Importantly, technology does not judge people for their sensory or learning issues. Technology does not exclude, look down on, or rate people. Technology only does what it is told to do.

The third lesson was that during the first college project looking at the range of people's access needs, I found it easier to support by separating functions and apps according to type of media. These forms of media, however, weren't necessarily used according to the students' access issues. Instead, media preferences were made according to what they wanted to do, the kind of learning and communication they felt comfortable with, and the trends of using tablets or cell phones.

Fourth, small changes that mobile technologies can provide can lead to fundamental changes that improve people's lives considerably. What's more, given initial skills, people with access needs often develop many more skills on their own.

For instance, given their existing skills in using discussion forums, the students involved in the first study skills project preferred using discussion boards to develop more skills. They shared tips and apps they'd found among themselves, and they gave one another advice on how to use their devices and set them up for different access needs. In this way, people are at their best when they are developing their own access, and people with access needs know more about their own issues than anyone else.

Using these lessons, I evaluated the main three tasks—taking notes, recording voices and sounds, and using touch and gestures—that were most useful and cell phones and tablets are best designed to be used for.[5] Each of these are discussed shortly, presented first as Apple functions followed by Android functions.

What I'm not going to do, though, is give you precise menus and where to find them. Apple and Android have a habit of keeping me awake at night by changing these menus on a regular basis, and a dollar to a hundred they will have done so again by the time this book is published.

So, what I have done in this book is give you pointers about the functions that will still be available, leaving you to do a little more homework to find out where they are.

APPS AND FUNCTIONS FOR ACCESSING WRITING AND TYPING

There are many ways of using mobile technologies for note-taking and organizational tasks. During our work to provide support, my colleagues and I found that people like to write on paper or type quick notes into memo-writing apps.

For those we work with, lists are also particularly important, as access needs often mean you have to organize yourself more. For reading and writing this text, we found that Apple provides features for supporting people with sight issues and certain forms of dyslexia higher on the spectrum for typing information or reading others' handwriting.

For instance, regular book text, icons, menus, and note-taking text in memo-writing, calendar, or word-processing apps can be increased through Apple's accessible preferences. In addition, pages of text can often be zoomed in or out of using pinches and gestures or expanding hands while holding fingers on the touch screen.

These functions mostly must be set up when getting the mobile technology first, but they can be easily customized for an individual's needs. Similarly, we've found that different Braille options through different wireless networking functions, such as Bluetooth devices, allow for contracted and eight-dot Braille.

Similarly, color-inversion options in the accessibility preferences menu (and remarkably through novelty apps such as Photo Booth) can make it easier to read text and some images. For instance, changing light-colored backgrounds to darker colors and darker-colored text to lighter colors can make reading text or even recognizing text easier.

Interestingly, we've found that enabling this function on our own machines through accessible settings also strains our eyes less if we are reading prose and notes for a long time. After inverting colors, we've also found there were fewer light points to focus on in pages and apps providing stickies, and it allowed us more power to transform numerous daily note-taking and organizational tasks.

However, as it took time to investigate, set up, and enable the features, we've found using generic novelty apps also allowed transformation of single pages, if you want to change a picture quickly.

For example, an X-ray option inverted the colors of text and its background, making handwriting photographed using this app more readable—

although this accessible function was not a design feature of the app and is not advertised.

Perhaps the most fascinating example of this feature I found was during the photography short course using mobile technologies. At the end of the first day, I switched on Photo Booth on my iPad, put it in X-ray mode, and held it over a page of handwritten notes from the class for a man who was registered blind. After looking at the page for a few seconds, he turned to me amazed, then he memorably told me this was the first handwriting he'd seen in years.

Android has a similar approach to Apple's. Android has a mix of possible functions that can help with note-taking and organization or with reading similar text in documents. Some of the features that exist are standard and just involve making text, cursors, and the like larger. However, some separate accessible features are more specialized, and so they are accessed via a special menu in settings or through custom apps you'll have to download.

Android's main instrument of inclusion is magnification gestures. This function allows you to pan across an image or a page by dragging your fingers across the screen, to zoom into an image or page by reverse pinching or unpinching your fingers, and to return to the regular view state by lifting fingers off the screen—as I write, this gesture needs two fingers to work, but it is best to check depending on when you're reading.

With Android, you can also magnify standard-size text through repeatedly tapping the same point of the touch screen gently—as I write, this is three taps, but again please check to see if this is still the same. Android systems also include test utilities that allow you to personalize settings according to your own access needs.

For instance, these settings allow people with visual access needs to automatically adjust their color settings by means of an initial set-up test. The results of this test become part of your profiles and allow you to adjust your future use through these personal color preferences.

Android also provides accessible text for people with hearing loss. For instance, you can use Google subtitles, which are a form of closed captions for videos that support this feature when played through an Android app, such as YouTube. The language, text size, and color of text and background can be adjusted for this setting by means of a slider.

RECORDING VOICES AND OTHER SOUNDS USING APPS AND FUNCTIONS

In our work, my colleagues and I found Apple's accessible audio functions are currently among its weakest features. Although, the most helpful functions we've used are speech-to-text and vice versa, which have improved a great deal lately, especially with the rise of Siri.

Perhaps rather obviously, most of these speech-to-text functions we use are most useful for those who have visual issues and learning difficulties, who often prefer voice notes to writing. Helpfully, we also found settings could be changed. These options included the speed of speech—with many people with visual issues preferring faster speech and some people with learning difficulties preferring slower speech—and dialect and language options such as US English and accents.

Usefully, we found that people with hearing and visual issues, which was quite common among older people, could adjust the phonetics and pitch to make the voice more pronounced. However, the settings were complicated to change and took a great deal of investigation for those we supported, as the apps had to be adjusted and applied individually—there was no *one-size-fits-all* tip we could tell them about.

My colleagues and I also found that the computerized voice singled out the users in public, a feature that could prove embarrassing and highlighted their access needs to those around them. However, most of those who used these functions also used headphones, which nullified most of their embarrassment, particularly as it is common for most cell phone users to have these nowadays.

Despite a lack of audio functions, Apple has apps such as QuickTime Player that are useful for recording long notes, tours, talks, or classes. The files from these recordings can also be easily saved, stored, and transferred to other machines with other operating systems and listened to.

During our first project, we also trial tested extra apps such as Evernote to record lectures and notes. This app filed and displayed sound recordings easily, and it could be used to store graphics and make written notes alongside these recordings. These apps also had the advantage of being able to automatically store some files on the cloud. These files could then be downloaded by Evernote and loaded onto another machine. This was a helpful feature of the app for us, and storage and ease of access were important to those we supported.

Like QuickTime Player, with Evernote the machine we loaded our sound files onto didn't have to be Apple, and recordings could be listened to and renamed easily. However, we also found that the sound files in Evernote were difficult to remove from the actual app and be played by a different app.

Android also had text-to-speech functions with settings that could be adjusted for speed, language, and clarity—in this way, both systems seemed to be similar, although equally as limited. Similarly, we also tended to rely on Android's voice-recording apps to support people in lectures, when creating notes, and for reviewing longer information that needed to be stored.

Like Apple, Android made it easy to record, file, and store notes for people with visual issues and learning difficulties. As the features were easy to learn and available to all users, they supported a large number of users in lectures and during tours. These notes could also be heard back through other apps and machines.

Where voices were recorded on Android's own apps, we found that files could be edited using the same app's functions. This made it useful for people with hearing as well as visual issues. Interestingly, this also made it useful for me too, with my hearing access needs.

For instance, in lectures, meetings, and tours I often recorded voices then played them back later as I would regularly miss certain words here and there. After having used this function with others, I found listening later helped me recap information at a higher volume.

We also found that Android apps had the advantage of creating files that could be organized using folders or uploading to regular Android-based cloud apps, such as Google Drive. With Google overseeing Android, these apps seemed to work well together.

TAKING PHOTOGRAPHS AND RECORDING VIDEOS USING APPS AND FUNCTIONS

My colleagues and I felt photography was particularly helpful and enjoyable during support sessions as a way of learning, recording information and memories, and bonding with others. This was why I later helped to develop a photography short course with other colleagues, as it turned out that photography could also develop other "soft skills" and confidence.

Apart from reversing the colors as per the text settings discussed earlier, on Apple devices we found that the regular camera app or Photo Booth were again largely accessible without making too many changes. These apps also appeared to have powerful regular functions for those, for example, with visual issues, such as zooming into class boards, artworks, or regular graphics.

The files containing these images were also often shared by social media sites—through closed messages or groups—or via cloud networks such as iCloud to help colleagues or others with visual issues or learning disabilities.

Consequently, although this was not their regular function, by accident these apps quickly became our augmented zoom device of choice.

Apple's regular camera app also has a video option built in, so my colleagues and I could switch from still photographs to recording movies quickly in cultural places. We also found the time-lapse function in the camera allowed us to record segments of classes or tours in semi-real time using a smaller size of file. Students found they could zoom into these images on screen later for revision or use video-recording and editing apps to zoom into details.

Whether in class or cultural places, we had to get permission and check what images and places we could record—this was especially important in galleries that often have rules on photography. These images could not be shared online, published, or broadcast in any other way.

During our work, we have found that videoing is useful for those with learning difficulties and hearing issues too.

For example, video conferencing allows easier communication between classes or tours, when people with learning difficulties need most backup and help with organization. Videoing is also useful for sign-language conversations, tutorials, or real-time translation in class, and it makes it easier to lip-read when playing back classes or tours.

Android's camera settings and gallery functions are similar to Apple's in structure and function, although Android's camera does not have time-lapse photography. The images are similar, however, and can be filed and edited in the same way, although because Android is on many devices the quality of the camera may vary and have extra camera features.

USING TOUCH AND GESTURES SETTINGS

During our work supporting people with access needs, my colleagues and I often found that touch functions on cell phones and tablets were the hardest for users to get used to. What's more, we also discovered that many people we supported were often put off from using their mobile technologies when they first got them. However, once our users stuck with learning their gestures, these functions provided a powerful skill they could use on other technologies, and encouraged them to learn more skills through mobile technologies.

Apple's assistive-touch feature allows users to design their own custom gestures; this supports people with issues of limb mobility to record simple gestures to replace complex ones. In our work, we also found this feature particularly useful for people with higher-on-the-spectrum learning difficulties, who may find learning sensory-motor skills more difficult.

After these gestures are recorded, they are available through favorites on the device menu, and they provide an easier means of navigating Apple devices, recording notes and classes, and recording videos and images.

A downside we found to Apple's assistive touch is that if simple gestures are needed because people cannot manage more complex gestures, this setup requires supporters to record and match both gestures. You have to record the complex gesture and match it to the simpler custom gesture.

With Apple mobile technologies, it's also possible to set up guided access that locks a multi-use tablet on a single app. This function enables people with access needs to ensure a particular app is always available without having to tap its icon. However, as with custom gestures this function needs supporters to adjust the settings, meaning it is difficult to initially set up.

This issue is changing, though. As the years have passed, voice commands through apps such as Siri ameliorate our need for certain gestures and make accessing certain functions easier. Although Siri also needs a degree of training, this training is easier for people with many access needs, although of course Siri needs more support for people with hearing and communication issues.

Android's custom touch gestures were found to be broadly similar to Apple's. For instance, Android allowed users to control the speed, simplicity, or complexity of gestures, although these still often require supporters to adjust the system's settings.

Importantly, Android also allows its users to access numerous apps and functions through its voice inputs, just as it does its voice-to-text functions. However, those we have supported could not use or found it more difficult to use voice functions to organize files, conduct complex web searches—or type in website names—or use camera functions.

SUMMARY

My colleagues and I, who have supported people with access needs using mobile technologies, found that Apple and Android had similar access settings. Both types of mobile technology also improved the skills people need to access cultural places. These skills include accessing information, recording and taking notes in lectures and tours, and taking images that can be studied in greater detail later.

For instance, during trials both Apple and Android allowed users to enlarge text, reverse colors, and save and change video files in order to increase their quality or ease of storage. These mobile technologies consequently have the potential to increase the enjoyment and learning during visits to places such as the museums, theaters, and monuments that are written about later.

However, there are some functions that make Apple and Android devices less useable in preparing for or having tours of cultural places. For instance, developing filing structures using text commands was more difficult or occasionally complex to access for people with higher-on-the-spectrum learning difficulties.

In addition, we often found it difficult to access wireless networks inside cultural places like museums and theaters, particularly in preserved historical buildings with thick walls.

Consequently, people with access needs and those who support them must evaluate systems according to their own needs, skills, and purposes of visiting cultural places. They must also judge which functions are important for their needs, given their context and environment.

However, it also needs to be borne in mind that these mobile technologies are evolving. The more you use these systems as a means of support, the more likely you will have the skills to take advantage of new technologies when they appear.

Section II

Twelve Cities

This section describes twelve large cities that are great to visit, either for a day or for a vacation. That's one for every month of the year, if you have the time and inclination.

As I wrote in the introduction, these cities and cultural places were chosen largely according to a five-step plan, based on my previous research on this topic and supporting people in education and cultural places. It's appropriate at this point to remind you about the five-step plan.

THE FIVE-STEP PLAN

In my work, I've found some cultural places have two or three steps to provide access, and this provides some support for people visiting these places. These steps may help people who are often lower on the spectrum of access needs have an enjoyable visit, although much of what can be done is still missed.

For instance, a museum may have a ramp outside, Braille labels next to exhibits, and an ASL tour in its galleries. Similarly, a theater may have automatically opening doors at the front, ways of traveling to different floors via elevators, and a website with accessible information. But this doesn't make these cultural places highly accessible.

The best access strategies in cultural places think about what I've found to be at least five individual steps to help people get fuller access, no matter their access needs. This being said, there are more steps given particular circumstances and highly specialized access needs, where people will need other forms of access too. This could include medical help, for instance, and it should be noted that no cultural place can cover all access needs, as new ones arise all the time.

However, no matter who we are, there seem to be five core steps[1] that provide effective access for most people, no matter their level or type of access needs. These five steps are (1) the ability to go to places with people we know or meet *people we feel comfortable with* through these cultural places; (2) the chance to *learn* while we are in our cultural places; (3) access to *information and information technologies* that will help us get to, get around, learn from, or just enjoy a cultural place; (4) the ability to be in as many of the public *places and spaces* as possible in a cultural place, either in person or through the Web; and (5) the ease of access to *mobility* to search for information, to learn, to go around with someone we know, or to be able to travel around all the public spaces that are available.

For instance, I have few access needs, so I find it relatively easy to go to a museum or a theater with my wife and children, Nick and Fia, as long as the exhibition or play is appropriate. When I get to these places, I'm mostly able to learn about the artworks or learn something interesting from the performance I watch without too much difficulty, as long as I have sight of whoever's speaking.

I can physically get to most galleries in most museums or the main auditoria of most theaters. I also find it easy to get to the bathroom, café, and shops of most museums, monuments, and theaters. So, I can access the public spaces of most cultural places, and I have the mobility to find information online and to learn in different places. I'm also mobile enough to enjoy myself, and most of my friends and family are mobile enough to join me in these cultural places and enjoy themselves too.

However, people higher on the spectrum of access needs, such as my older relatives, friends, or those I have supported, may need many more adjustments than I do according to these five steps as a minimum.

For example, when I was at the Met, my friend and colleague who headed access at the museum, Rebecca Maginnis, covered all five steps. She made sure verbal imaging sessions included friends or family members. She made sure people visiting the Met had the opportunity of learning no matter who they were (the museum has highly developed courses and a whole education wing). Information around the Met was available in different formats, such as large print and audio for people who found reading regular text harder. And finally, the spaces in the Met, such as galleries and the education wing, had lifts, flat surfaces, and wide doors. A great deal of thought was given to getting to practical places, such as the museum spaces, bathrooms, and cafés. Thought was also given to how people navigated the website to find information and learn. Consequently, the Met could be said to have adapted to provide a sophisticated and highly planned form of access.

HOW THE CITIES AND CULTURAL
PLACES WERE CHOSEN

The choice of cities in this book is based on a survey of accessibility in the cultural places in each city, and the general public access in the places themselves. The process for choosing the cities and cultural places was rigorous, and I have tried to balance places with interesting arts and culture with places that provide good if not great accessibility. These decisions were made according to three choices.

The first choice was the popularity of the cities' metropolitan areas—that is to say, they are some of the most visited cities in the US according to tour listings[2]—and the strength of their arts scene. In these cities, I've found strong and voluminous public art collections in museums, galleries, and theaters, and regular plays, musicals, and movies in their theaters and performance centers.

The second choice was their distribution across the US, representing the north, south, east, west, and middle of the country. It's true that the Northeast and the West Coast are particularly well represented, as they have a high concentration of some of the largest cities in the US. However, care was also taken to choose cities that represent diverse populations, cultures, and traditions in the southern states and the heartland of the US too—these cultures and traditions can include social, outdoor, and musical events, as well as exhibitions and festivals.

The third choice was to find cities that were relatively accessible by public transportation or car and had largely accessible transport and road networks once you get to them. This doesn't mean that their transport network is perfect, or that you can get out of a metro station and get straight into a museum or theater—some of the biggest cities in particular are difficult to get around and their metro stops are miles apart. But the ability to get accessible transportation and to be dropped off at the cultural place was certainly an important consideration in the selection process.[3]

In this section, there is a chapter for each city, and each chapter is laid out in the same way, describing access for visitors with vision loss, hearing loss, learning difficulties, memory loss, and mobility issues, as well as for supporters.

Importantly, I've tried to be curatorial about which cultural places were included in each chapter, and in which order I presented each cultural place. That is to say, I've approached choosing these places in the same way that a curator in a museum would create an exhibition of artworks, by hanging or placing them in an order that follows a reasonable pattern.

The cultural places in this section figure highly on the five steps of the plan for at least some needs. For instance, while looking at all these cultural places I've found many focus on meeting spots for people with higher-on-the-spectrum autism or for people with dementia. What's more, I've found that most places think mostly of Braille, audio description, and captioning when providing information for people with vision or hearing loss. This is largely to be expected and plays to people's most essential access needs.

Unfortunately, I couldn't include all accessible cultural places in each city as this would take several volumes. I've also had to leave out a few cultural places that are great accessible places but whose access may not cover all five steps or who were in cities packed with too many places to mention.

In my picks, I've had to be particularly disciplined about how I made my choices in cities like New York, Boston, and Washington, DC, as I felt like a kid in a candy shop in these cities. This means that the cultural places that have made "the cut" in these chapters are ones that are not just high on the five-point plan but also have what I think are the most interesting collections. They are the most iconic cultural places in these cities, and are often places that represent the US to the rest of the world.

Consequently, I've tried to go into some depth about each place and choose a mixture of art museums, science museums, monuments, and theaters in each city. With a few exceptions, I've chosen four museums or monuments and two top theaters or performance centers for each city.

Last, it should be noted that this book does not have reviews for each cultural place. This book does not try to emulate TripAdvisor or some other travel guides that give opinion pieces based on the access needs or the preferences or tastes of visitors or customers.

In this choice of cities and cultural places, I only give information about the services that are available and advertised at the time of writing. You will have your own preferences, and the information I provide is designed only as a starting point for your own preparation for visiting these places. It is also strongly advised that you contact the places yourself to arrange your visit if you wish to get the most out of it.

Chapter Six

Atlanta, Georgia

Traveling through Georgia, I think of it as a traditional southern state. I think of *Gone with the Wind*, Savannah, woods and alligators, great music from singers such as Otis Redding, and great civil rights leaders, most famously Rev. Dr. Martin Luther King Jr. However, Atlanta is a surprisingly young city for such a traditional state, founded as recently as 1837 as the terminal point of the Atlantic railway company's line. This modernity is now reflected in its tall downtown city center, which hosts the headquarters of world-famous companies such as Coca-Cola and CNN, and its place as a transport hub for road, rail, and air.

INSIDER TIP

When I first visited Georgia, it was to stay with my closest friends, whose family was based on one of its air bases. I hadn't considered going to Atlanta, and if it wasn't for my Greyhound route, it probably still wouldn't be a place I would have stopped over. To me, it was a corporate hub with little on my bucket list. However, I've now realized that to miss out on Atlanta would've been a real shame.

In my opinion, the central district, downtown Atlanta, is an accessible icon of modern American culture, facing the rest of the world as much as it faces its neighboring states. It has a number of user-friendly sidewalks and a cosmopolitan glass-and-steel feeling that contrasts with the local buzz of its rolling, elegant suburban surroundings. It is also a generously spread-out city center, with attractions, museums, and theaters relatively close to one another. This center has sophisticated modern neighborhoods and an arts and science scene, plus restaurants, bars, diners, and cafés that mirror its dynamic population.

It should also be understood that greater Atlanta itself is not so big, with a surprisingly small population of around 420,000 people within its city limits. However, the shape of the city belies a much larger suburban non-Atlanta area that surrounds the city, so you wouldn't know you're leaving Atlanta's city limits without consulting your map.

The six accessible sites chosen for your Atlanta tour are as follows:

The High Museum of Art (The High)

High Museum of Art
1280 Peachtree St NE
Atlanta, GA 30309
Tel: 404 733 4400

The museum has more than 15,000 artworks, part of which is a significant collection of works by artists from southern states of the US. Since its inception, The High has also amassed a large collection of nineteenth- and twentieth-century American art, a significant element of which is African American art, classical European paintings, and contemporary art, photography, and folk art from around the world. The museum itself was founded in 1905 and has been based in a stately home on the city's Peachtree Street since 1926.

The Martin Luther King, Jr. National Historical Park (The Park)

Administration: 450 Auburn Ave NE
Atlanta, GA 30312
Tel: 404 331 5190

The Park is a site of almost thirty-five acres of living history. It is based around the buildings from the late nineteenth and early twentieth century that represented the life of the Rev. Dr. Martin Luther King Jr. Many of the houses in the Park's campus are traditional clapboard with gabled roofs and represent whole blocks in the Sweet Auburn district of Atlanta. The Visitor Center acts as the *de facto* hub of the Park, which includes the home where King himself was born, and is said to date from 1895. The park also contains this neighborhood and King's earliest church, the Ebenezer Baptist Church, where his father and grandfather ministered. King's home was listed on the US National Register of Historic Places in 1974, and the Park was established as a national park in 1980.

World of Coca-Cola at Pemberton Place®

121 Baker St NW

Atlanta, GA 30313
Tel: 404 676 5151

World of Coca-Cola® is a twenty-acre campus on Pemberton Place, Atlanta, close to where Coca-Cola was first developed. The campus is designed to tell the story of the development of this drink and one of the US's best-known companies. World of Coca-Cola features around five hundred sparkling and still cola brands from more than two hundred countries, Coca-Cola collectibles, exhibits from Coca-Cola's history including its 130-year-old formula, and its bottling process. Visitors to the site can also taste over one hundred beverages and meet its mascot, the seven-foot-tall Coca-Cola Polar Bear. World of Coca-Cola's site was opened in 1990 and was dedicated to the pharmacist, John S. Pemberton, who first formulated Coca-Cola in 1886.

Children's Museum of Atlanta (Children's Museum)

275 Centennial Olympic Park Dr NW
Atlanta, GA 30313
Tel: 404 659 5437

Children's Museum is a charitable organization dedicated to child develop ment through interactive, hands-on, problem-solving exhibitions, displays, and activities. It is aimed primarily at children from birth to eight years old, and it also conducts community outreach and educational programs in schools. Its programs are designed to stimulate imagination, criticality, discovery, and learning and to encourage artistic expression through the use of as many senses as possible. It is bright and noisy and very tactile. There is eating space, and the spaces encourage family interaction. The museum itself is relatively modern, having opened in 2003.

The Fox Theatre (The Fox)

660 Peachtree St NE
Atlanta, GA 30308
Tel: 404 881 2100
Box Office Tel: 855 285 8499

The Fox is a live concert and theater venue, featuring a range of styles, genres, and periods of music and entertainment. It hosts the Mighty Mo, whose 3,622 pipes comprise the largest Möller theater organ in the world. Since its early years, the architecture of the Fox has also been lavish, attempting to re-create the designs of Far Eastern temples and mosque-style domes, minarets, and archways. The interior design is equally opulent, featuring gold leaf, luxurious textiles, wall and ceiling paintings with optical illusions, turreted ceilings, stained glass windows, a red-carpet entryway, and gilt work. The Fox opened in 1929 as a movie theater and was leased to William Fox, after whom the theater is named. The opening movie was Disney's *Steamboat Willie* with Mickey Mouse. Its opulence caused early financial problems however, and in 1932 William Fox declared bankruptcy. Following this bankruptcy, the theater was auctioned on Atlanta's courthouse steps for $75,000, expanded its shows, and featured live performances as well as movies.

Ferst Center for the Arts, Georgia Tech (The Ferst)

349 Ferst Dr NW
Atlanta, GA 30332-0468
Tel: 404 894 9600 or 404 894 2787
Administration in the Office of the Arts
353 Ferst Dr NW, Suite 233
Atlanta, GA 30332-0468

The Ferst is a modern performing arts center on the campus of Georgia Institute of Technology. It has a large site with auditoria and exhibition spaces, and although it is based in a college it's not far from the city center. The center is run from the college through the Georgia Tech Arts Advisory Board, alumni, artists, and community leaders and follows the arts culture and policies of the campus. This means that it runs shows you'll probably be less likely to find in regular theaters. The Ferst also advocates for students, faculty, administration, community members, and professional artists through its artworks and partner arts research developed at Georgia Tech. At the time of writing, the Ferst is featuring arts@tech, with artists from across the globe performing in the center on disability, interconnectivity, and mobility design.

ACCESS FOR VISITORS WITH SIGHT LOSS

The High allows visitors to bring magnifiers for gallery wall labels and runs docent-led verbal description tours and tactile exploration during selected tours. If you want to attend a tour, I'd advise that you contact the museum at least a month before you plan to visit for more information about these tours and to book. Alternatively, if you have a group of fifteen or more adults or a school group of ten or more, contact Adult Group Tours or School Tours at the museum, mentioning your access needs at least a month before you plan to visit.

   The Park has accessible information on the history of the area and the work of Rev. Dr. Martin Luther King Jr. on its website, which is designed to be accessible to screen readers and zoom functions (https://www.nps.gov/

malu/siteindex.htm). In addition, the Park has trained park rangers, committed to providing bespoke inclusion according to individual access needs. With this in mind, I'd advise that you contact the Park at least a month before you plan to visit about arranging accessible information or a ranger's support on the day.

World of Coca-Cola has a number of accessible documents available for those with vision loss visiting its campus. For instance, they offer Braille guide maps at ticket windows and Guest Services, and mobile text and audio technologies from Guest Services that can be used in exhibitions. World of Coca-Cola also has the Explorer app for Apple devices and a website that offers mostly accessible information and activities on the history of the drink (https://www.worldofcoca-cola.com/plan-your-visit/world-coca-cola-explorer-mobile-app/).

Children's Museum has accessible resources and can make what it describes as *reasonable modifications* for programs or meetings. They state you'll need to contact them at least a week before you plan to visit to ask for these services or to tell them about specific needs and information. Call 404 527 3694 or Georgia Relay Service Access: 711.

ACCESS FOR VISITORS WITH HEARING LOSS

The High captions a number of its videos that are shown throughout its galleries, particularly those it produces itself. The museum also has free, borrowable assistive listening devices for its auditorium, which can be checked out at the entrance. The High also provides ASL interpreters for a number of its talks and lectures, which are advertised on its calendar or through its website. I'd advise you contact the access department for information before you visit. Call 404 733 4575 or email access@high.org.

The Park has information on its website about its buildings, neighborhoods, and streets that can be read as you go around (https://www.nps.gov/malu/siteindex.htm). You can also contact the Park directly to ask about ASL interpretation for tours or ask for support from park rangers. For more information about access or to ask for support, use the regular number for the Park: 404 331 5190.

World of Coca-Cola offers paid VIP guided tours that can be tailored for some visitors with hearing loss, depending on access needs. The site also has borrowable headsets to help hear the tour guide and has previously arranged for ASL interpreters, although these are not widely advertised. These tours are limited to ten visitors or fewer, and I'd advise you to contact the site at least a month in advance if possible to arrange support for your tour or find out if support can be arranged before booking it. World of Coca-Cola also has captioning that is projected onto a panel in front of visitors for videos in some theaters and presentations. The captioning devices need to be arranged before you visit the site, and I'd advise contacting them about this at least two weeks before you visit. Call 404 676 5151.

Children's Museum also advertises *reasonable modifications* for visitors with hearing loss, as well as a provision for alternate formats of information and educational materials. Call 404 527 3694 or TDD/TTY 711. I would advise calling the museum at least two weeks before you plan to visit.

The Fox has a range of free, borrowable assisted listening devices for all its shows. To use one, you'll need to leave official photo ID with the theater during your visit. Contact the Guest Experience Manager on the general number for more information at 404 881 2100. The Fox also advertises some ASL-interpreted Sunday matinees for shows that have a long run. If you need an ASL interpreter for a regular show however, call the box office two weeks or more before you plan to visit to find out if this is possible.

The Ferst has an assistive listening system. Contact the box office or the administration offices before you plan to visit. Call 404 894 9600.

ACCESS FOR VISITORS WITH LEARNING DISABILITIES, MEMORY LOSS, AND AUTISM HIGHER ON THE SPECTRUM

The High has a sensory room equipped with fidgets, a crash pad, and noise-canceling headphones for visitors with autism higher on the spectrum. These headphones and fidgets can also be borrowed for art-making workshops. The High has a monthly tour called Musing Together that's run by the Georgia Chapter of the Alzheimer's Association. I'd advise contacting them at least a month before you plan to visit for information and to book. Call 404 733 4575 or email access@high.org. The tours themselves are led by teaching artists, and medicines and supplies are permitted for those who need them. The High also has social stories for visitors with learning disabilities and autism higher on the spectrum to familiarize themselves with the museum before they visit, which are available in English and Spanish. Again, contact the access department.

At **World of Coca-Cola**, many of the exhibits and shows are easy to understand and sensorially accessible to visitors with learning difficulties as they are multimedia and interactive. Good examples of interactive exhibits and shows at the time of writing include *In Search of the Secret Formula* multisensory movie and the Pop Culture Gallery. However, these exhibits can be very stimulating for visitors with autism higher on the spectrum or epilepsy.

Children's Museum has a social guide called *My Visit to The Children's Museum of Atlanta*, which features a step-by-step narrative for visitors on parts of the museum such as the learning zones and programs. These guides are largely for visitors with learning difficulties and autism higher on the spectrum, and they are available in binders from the front and learning zones. The museum also has a special session on the first Saturday of each month for children with autism higher on the spectrum, allowing them to tour in their own time in a calm, relaxed environment with their families. Call 404 527 3694 or Georgia Relay Service Access 711 to ask for these services or about specific needs and information.

ACCESS FOR VISITORS WITH MOBILITY ISSUES

Although **The High** doesn't have a parking garage, visitors with mobility issues can find accessible spaces at the nearby Woodruff Arts Center parking garage if you have a disability badge on your automobile. The parking garage also has access spaces for larger vehicles for people with access needs. At The High, there is elevator access to the main museum entrance from the Arts Center MARTA station, which is the local light railway, and from the parking garage. It has close drop-off spots on the street outside and a wide doorway instead of revolving doors at its main entrance. The museum states that visitors can use their own mobility devices in the public areas of the museum, and seating is provided throughout the galleries for people who need to rest frequently. The museum also has free, borrowable wheelchairs. The museum's security offices can help you get these if you leave official photo ID until they're returned.

The Park has accessible spaces close to the visitor center entrance of its parking lot for people with disability badges on their automobiles. The parking lot itself has paved walkways, and the visitor center is single level on the ground floor with accessible entrance doors—although it should be noted that the restroom doors are manual. The first and second floors of King's birth home are accessible, with a stair lift to the second floor, and there are wide walkways to the rear. Park rangers can also provide a photo tour for those who can't access parts of the building. The sales outlet has ramps and paved walkways leading to them, the historic fire station has an elevator to its second level, and the Baptist church has a portable ramp. The Park also has free borrowable wheelchairs at the visitor center, although these need to be returned half an hour before it closes. I'd recommend calling The Park on its main number before you visit for information: 404 331 5190.

World of Coca-Cola has a parking garage with accessible spaces for automobiles with disability badges, and you can use your own mobility devices around the site. They also have borrowable wheelchairs, although as with other sites you'll need to leave official photographic ID with the museum until they're returned.

Children's Museum states its entire site, including bathrooms and fountains, are accessible for people with mobility issues, and visitors can use their own mobility devices around the museum. The museum also has an accessible wheelchair entrance with electronic doors, elevators for Step Up to Science, and ramps in parts of Gateway to the World.

The Fox has accessible parking spaces in the parking lots nearby for automobiles with disability badges, and parking attendants can direct you to these. Outside the theater, there are also accessible curbs. I'd advise calling the theater for information about bookable parking at least a week before you visit: 404 881 2016. The Fox also has an accessible ticket office and concession stands, plus an elevator to higher floors. In the auditorium, they have accessible seating available to be booked and a small number of borrowable wheelchairs. You can even arrange for someone to help you from the street outside to your seat. I'd advise you contact the venue at least a month before you plan to visit to get information about booking and support.

Being set on a college campus, the area around **The Ferst** is largely accessible. There is a generally flat sidewalk and ramp to the site, a drop-off point not far away, and wide accessible doorways at the entrance. Inside its site, the center states it is largely accessible to people with mobility issues, and it has accessible seating. Some performances also have a disability theme, for those interested in this topic. Further access needs can be discussed with the center's administration office, and I'd advise you call them at least two weeks before you visit to discuss the support you'll need: 404 894 2787.

ACCESS FOR SUPPORTERS

At **The High**, families are welcome to use the Sensory Room free of charge, and a staff member can direct you to the room.

The Park is designed largely for school or adult groups or families, with a trail that can be followed independently or toured with park rangers.

At the time of writing, **The Ferst** is showcasing performances that include issues related to disability. Georgia Institute of Technology also advertises public artworks around its campus, most of which are interactive and accessible to touch. Information about each public artwork can be found on its website (https://arts.gatech.edu/content/visualartstech).

Chapter Seven

Boston, Massachusetts

Boston predates the US Constitution by more than a century. It was founded in the early seventeenth century by a colony of Puritan Protestants who sailed from Plymouth, a city in Devon, England, after which Plymouth Rock was named. For this reason, the city and its surrounding smaller cities, such as Cambridge, have a traditional reputation as the intellectual home of the US— so much of the country's academic, religious, and political history came from this founding community that it became known as the *Cradle of Liberty*. This image abides today and, despite its largely modern downtown area and cutting-edge technology labs, it still has a large number of older buildings and a traditional old-city layout at its core. Boston and its outlying cities are also still home to some of the most famous colleges in the US like Harvard, Massachusetts Institute of Technology (MIT), Tufts, and Boston University. It can be said that it is one of the US's cultural meccas.

INSIDER TIP

When I think of accessible venues in Boston, the first thing that comes to mind is our museums. The Museum of Fine Arts (MFA) has an incredible program for making art accessible to people with vision loss. While they run a regular, monthly program, they are also very open to setting up private tours. They need at least a week to identify an available volunteer. . . . The Museum of Science employs an accessibility specialist who is blind, and they have offered a wide range of accessible exhibits over the years. Examples have included movement patterns used by birds in flight, a replica of a spider's web, and a lightning generator guaranteed to impress blind and sighted folks alike. Both museums are accessible. I would be remiss if I did not mention the variety of trolley tours available in Boston. They all offer narrated historic tours of the city.

—Jerry Berrier, Educationalist, Boston, personal correspondence,
October 2019

The six accessible sites chosen for your Boston tour are as follows:

Boston Museum of Fine Arts (Boston MFA)

Avenue of the Arts
465 Huntington Ave
Boston, MA 02115
Tel: 617 267 9300

Boston MFA is perhaps the most comprehensive regional art museum in the Northeast, set in a traditional colonnaded building in the Fenway area of Boston. The museum is also an intellectual hub, hosting the School of the Museum of Fine Arts, Boston, which is now part of Tufts University's School of Arts and Sciences. Boston MFA's main collections include artworks from the US, the Americas, Europe, Asia, Africa, and Oceania. It also includes objects from ancient civilizations, including ancient Greece, Rome, and Egypt. Its collection is particularly large for a regional museum, with approximately half a million artworks and other objects. Boston MFA was founded in 1870 on a donated collection, with its building opening in 1876 on the US's centennial. The School of the Museum of Fine Arts was founded in the same year and has been among Boston's most important art colleges ever since. In 2010, the museum added new modern art and glass wings, including the Art of the Americas Wing.

The Isabella Stewart Gardner Museum (ISG)

25 Evans Way
Boston, MA 02115
Tel: 617 566 1401
information@isgm.org

ISG is based in a Venetian-style, palatial house built in 1903, modeled on the Palazzo Barbaro. It is located in the Fenway area of Boston, near other museums and Northeastern University. The museum's current collection includes botanicals in its walled garden, modern artworks, and musical instruments from the US, Europe, and Asia. The collection was founded by and is named after Isabella Stewart Gardner, the daughter of an early nineteenth-century Irish linen magnet. After inheriting a legacy from her family, Isabella and her husband transformed her small-scale collection into an encyclopedic collection and then the museum. The museum is still largely funded by Stewart Gardner's bequest, which was established on her death in 1924. The building is an integral feature of its collection and incorporates original windows, columns, and doorways from palaces in Italy. The building was expanded in 2004 with a new wing designed by the modernist Italian architect Renzo Piano.

Boston National Historical Park (Boston NHP)

21 Second Ave
Charlestown, MA 02129
Tel: 617 242 5601

Boston NHP is a national park that comprises a collection of various historical buildings and a shipyard, based on and around Boston's Inner Harbor and the River Charles. It is spread over forty-three acres of Charlestown, South Boston, and downtown and comprises different historical sites and their exhibits, including a naval tall ship. Most of its sites can be seen as you follow the Freedom Trail, and the park has two visitor centers in Faneuil Hall and Charlestown Navy Yard—this trail documents the Boston Tea Party, rallies, speeches, and characters that led to the American War of Independence. The site was originally a collection of different public buildings and was incorporated into the National Parks Service as a single site in 1974.

Boston Museum of Science (Boston MoS)

1 Science Park
Boston, MA 02114
Tel: 617 723 2500

Boston MoS features largely interactive exhibitions on a broad range of the natural sciences, engineering, and technology. It has a butterfly farm with live butterflies, a planetarium, an IMAX cinema, and performance space for live science shows by real scientists. It also has a broad range of temporary and touring exhibitions, which highlight real-world scientific applications as well as social issues. The museum has outreach and educational programs for the public and schools. It is designed for all age groups. The museum's collection, which included natural history specimens, was established in 1830 by the Boston Society of Natural History. However, the collection did not have a permanent home until 1864, when it opened as the New England Museum of Natural History in Boston's Back Bay. After World War II, it was renamed Boston Museum of Science, then the Museum of Science.

Boch Center, including The Wang and Shubert Theatres (The Boch)

270 Tremont St
Boston, MA 02116

Tel: 617 532 1255

The Boch is a not-for-profit arts center with two historic theaters on Tremont Street, Boston. It specializes in traditional performances of touring Broadway shows, theater, music concerts, dance performances, and opera. It also has shows by local community arts organizations. As I write, the center is developing the first Folk Americana Roots Hall of Fame, which will feature memorabilia and photographs. The highlight of the center is the Wang Theatre itself, which has a seating capacity of around 3,500 and is named on the National Register of Historic Places. The Wang opened in 1925 as a vaudeville music hall and movie theater, and its architecture and interiors were restored to their original standards in 1983. The theater has previously held shows by Ella Fitzgerald, Liza Minnelli, Queen, and more recently Lady Gaga.

Citizens Bank Opera House (The Opera House)

539 Washington St
Boston, MA 02111
Tel: 1 800 982 2787 or 617 259 3400

Although it has a smaller seating capacity of a little less than 2,700, the Opera House is similar to the Wang Theatre for its artistic and architectural importance. Its performances most importantly include Broadway touring shows, ballets, and comedies, and it also holds tours and academic talks. The building, which is registered with the Boston Landmarks Commission, is worth a visit too, as it was built and decorated in a French and Italianate style. The theater was originally opened for vaudeville shows in 1928, and was restored in the early millennium over the course of two years, which reduced its capacity. This restoration included gilding, marble inlays, murals, grand chandeliers, and heavy wooden paneling.

ACCESS FOR VISITORS WITH SIGHT LOSS

The MFA Guide is a borrowable audio description device at **Boston MFA** with around two hundred stops in English, can be checked out from the museum's front desk and has accessible information on its regular app. The museum also has art cards with raised line graphics of artworks, Braille or large-print documents, and audio-tactile interactive books. Ask about these devices at the museum's visitor center when you get there.

The museum also runs access programs for visitors with vision loss. For instance, *A Feeling for Form* includes tours for a range of ages—although these particularly appeal to adults—that feature tactile exploration, verbal description, and tactile graphics. The tours are free, but you'll need to preregister at least a week before the tour, although I'd recommend contacting them at least two weeks before you plan to visit. Call 617 369 3189 or email access@mfa.org. You'll also find more details about tours on the Boston MFA website.

ISG has special tour accommodations for people with sight loss by providing, for instance, a sighted guide. You'll need to ask for this support in advance. I'd advise contacting them at least two weeks before you plan to visit. Call 617 278 5147.

Boston NHP's official app and its Boston African American National Historic Site mobile app, both for Apple and Android, have largely accessible information and menus. The apps also feature an audio guided tour, *Trails to Freedom*, where visitors can hear about the history of the park's site and practical details such as opening hours. The app also has Boston's Freedom Trail® and Black Heritage Trail® with directions and estimated times between each stop, and a feature that can let you know your exact location in the park.

Boston MoS has audio labels around the museum, which allow you to hear what is normally printed. The museum's IMAX theater also features audio description for a number of its shows. More information can be found on its calendar of events, and devices playing this description can be taken from the information desk at the museum by leaving official photo ID until they're returned.

The museum's planetarium also has borrowable Braille constellation maps and tactile pictures. The information desk will have information about these when you visit, although it is always advisable to contact the museum before you visit to find out more. Call 617 723 2500 or email accessibility@mos.org. Boston MoS also offers sighted guide tours, where trained sighted guides lead verbal imaging tours for visitors with sight loss. Contact the museum at least two weeks before you plan to visit to arrange a tour. Call 617 589 3102.

Boch Center offers a number of audio-described performances for people with sight loss. Information about these performances can be found on their calendar or by emailing info@bochcenter.org. For the Wang Theatre, call 800 745 3000 or TTY: 800 943 4327. For the Shubert Theatre, call 866 300 9761 and TTY: 888 889 8587.

The Opera House offers visitors with low vision special seating with a more accessible view of the stage, and it has a number of audio-described shows. You can get more information about this and book these seats and shows through its calendar or box office. For more information about this support, email ADABoston@BroadwayInBoston.com.

ACCESS FOR VISITORS WITH HEARING LOSS

Boston MFA has borrowable assistive listening devices for gallery tours and talks and video guides for those who want to go around the museum by themselves. The museum also has headphones and hearing loops for people with adapted hearing aids in its auditoria. For more information about borrowing or using all these devices, contact the museum before you visit. Call 617 267 9300 or email access@mfa.org. The museum also has special programs and tours for people with hearing loss. For instance, *A Hand's Reach to Art* includes gallery tours, performances, and demonstrations in ASL.

ISG can provide ASL interpreters for regular group or individual tours of its museum. You'll need to contact the museum in advance for information and to book an interpreter. I'd advise you call at least a month before you plan to visit. Call 617 278 5147.

Boston MoS has borrowable assistive listening devices with headphones and neck loops, the latter for visitors with adapted hearing aids, which work around a large part of the museum. You can borrow these devices from the information desk by leaving official photo ID. I'd also advise you contact the museum before you arrive for more information about these devices. Call 617 723 2500 or email accessibility@mos.org.

Boston MoS's IMAX theater also has captioning, amplified narration, and show scripts for a number of its films and borrowable assistive listening devices and headsets. You can get these devices and information sources from ushers or the museum's box office, and the museum advises getting to the theater early to arrange for them in advance. The museum's planetarium can also arrange an ASL interpreter for its shows, although the museum asks that you request this from them at least two weeks before your visit. Call 617 723 2500 or email accessibility@mos.org.

The Boch has unique transliterated shows—shows where the dialogue is typed in real time. Check with the center or their calendar for these performances. For the Wang Theatre, call 800 745 3000 or TTY: 800 943 4327. For the Shubert Theatre, call 866 300 9761 or TTY: 888 889 8587 or email info@bochcenter.org.

The Opera House has borrowable assisted listening devices, ear speakers, or headphones that can be checked out in the main lobby or at coat check, although you'll need to rent them or leave official photo ID. For more information, email ADABoston@BroadwayInBoston.com. Some of their shows also have captions or ASL interpreters. Details of these can be found in their calendar or by contacting them directly via email at info@bostonoperahouse.com. In addition, it may be possible to ask directly for an ASL interpreter for the show you plan to visit. If you have an ASL request, the theater asks that you email them at least two weeks before you plan to visit and include "the language of ASL Request" in your subject line.

ACCESS FOR VISITORS WITH LEARNING DISABILITIES, MEMORY LOSS, AND AUTISM HIGHER ON THE SPECTRUM

Boston MFA runs a number of special programs for visitors with learning difficulties or memory loss. For example, its Access to Art program offers tours for groups of visitors including those with learning difficulties and memory loss, run by specially trained guides. Alternatively, Artful Adventures and Beyond the Spectrum are for groups of children and teens, including those with autism higher on the spectrum. These special programs mostly consist of tours of the gallery followed by making art, and the museum states that it can customize visits if asked to do so—this includes delivering it in Spanish. The museum also recognizes that some visitors with memory loss don't want to be part of a program, so the museum offers personalized tours for visitors with just their family, friends, or supporters. You'll need to arrange your participation in all these tours at least a month before you visit. Call 617 369 3302 or email access@mfa.org.

Boston NHP can support certain forms of learning disability in its education programs on an individual basis, its National Park Ranger programs in particular. You'll need to book these programs at least two weeks in advance, and I'd advise you tell the park about your learning needs when you do so. Call 617 242 5689. This notice will also allow park rangers to organize alternative materials and presentations. The park's Charlestown Navy Yard tours and classes can also arrange accessible and pre-visit materials given enough notice.

Boston MoS has audio labels that can speak text for those who find reading difficult. Ask the staff about these when you visit the museum.

ACCESS FOR VISITORS WITH MOBILITY ISSUES

Boston MFA has accessible spaces in their parking garage and lots in Museum Road and valet parking. It also has a drop-off area for people with mobility issues, and entrances have electronic doors. A number of the museum's galleries have seats, which can be used by visitors with mobility issues who need to rest. It also has free borrowable gallery stools for most exhibitions, which can be taken out by the visitor center—these stools are only allowed in special exhibitions with specific permission.

Most of the museum's bathrooms and eating spaces are largely accessible to visitors with mobility issues, and there is a specialized bathroom for wheelchair users by the visitor center. The museum also has a number of free borrowable manual wheelchairs and walkers with wheels, seats, and backrests at its entrance. The museum also recommends that visitors with mobility issues bring their own devices, and it states that its events are wheelchair accessible.

ISG has two accessible parking spaces on its site and a ramped loading zone that can be used for dropping off. Inside, the museum has elevators to all floors in the new building, largely accessible regular bathrooms, and special accessible restrooms in the New Wing. It also has a number of free borrowable wheelchairs, walkers, mobile seats, and canes at the admission desk. If you bring your own wheelchair, the museum states you may not be able to get through all doorways in the museum.

The museum can also make special accommodations for tours, musical performances, and lectures for those with mobility issues—these could include special group tours or regular tours. These accommodations need to be arranged before your visit. I'd recommend you get in touch with the museum at least a month before you plan to visit. Call 617 278 5147. Special accommodations can also be made for musical performances and lectures at ISG, including accessible seating or spaces if the museum is given enough notice. Again, I'd advise contacting them at least a month in advance. Call the box office at 617 278 5156. The museum also has a "Getting Around the Museum" webpage and brochure with detailed information.

Because it is a park based in a city, **Boston NHP** has varying levels of accessibility for visitors with mobility issues. The Freedom Trail, for example, has some of the oldest streets and neighborhoods in the city, so its sidewalks are narrow and uneven. However, there are regular curb-cuts and crosswalks at stoplights and signals. Many of the buildings along the trail only have stairs to upper floors, although there are occasional alternatives available, and Faneuil Hall has a ramp and elevator. It is advisable to contact the park before your visit to find the most mobility-friendly route. Call 617 242 5689. Getting to the park is relatively easier, however, as there are on-street accessible parking spaces for automobiles with disability badges, plus reserved accessible parking at Charlestown Navy Yard. For the latter, you will have to contact the park, I'd advise at least a week beforehand.

Boston NHP also has free borrowable wheelchairs that can be taken out for single-day use from the visitor centers. You will have to leave official photo ID as a deposit when you take them out until they're returned.

Boston MoS has accessible parking spaces for automobiles with disability badges in its parking garage. If these spaces are full, visitors may ask for permission to park in the museum's driveway on the day they visit. The museum also has a dropping-off and picking-up area near its automated entrance. The museum asserts that much of its gallery spaces are accessible to people with mobility issues. The museum also has wheelchair-accessible seating in its theaters and planetarium, along with a number of borrowable wheelchairs of varying sizes for adults and children, plus strollers and scooters, at the information desk.

Both **The Boch** and **The Opera House** are in the center of town near Tremont Street, close to the Boston T, the city's Metro. They both have parking garages they don't control nearby and areas where visitors can be dropped off close to their entrances, but Tremont is a busy street and you may have to exercise caution when doing so. Contact Boch Center before your visit, and it may be possible to arrange a person to meet you at the entrance if you are alone.

The Boch has accessible seating in The Wang and Shubert Theatres that can be booked at a range of prices depending on their closeness to the orchestra and stage. As the number of these seats is limited, I'd advise you contact the center at least a month before you plan to visit, even longer for popular shows. Call the Shubert Theatre at 866 300 9761 or TTY: 888 889 8587. Call the Wang Theatre at 800 745 3000 or TTY: 800 943 4327 or visit the box office. The Wang Theatre has an elevator from its lobby to all its upper levels and a disability lift to its lower lobby, and the Wang and Shubert Theatres both have partly accessible bathrooms. For more information to plan your visit, call 617 532 1255 or email stowers@bochcenter.org.

The Opera House has accessible and companion seats that can be booked. I'd advise you to contact the box office at least a month before you plan to visit, even longer before if the show you plan to see is popular. The theater has accessible bathrooms and an elevator to get to some but not all floors.

ACCESS FOR SUPPORTERS

Boston MFA has many events and programs that can be undertaken in groups or with supporters. For instance, Artful Adventures is for children and teens with their families, friends, and supporters. This program features art from different cultures and allows customized visits. The program itself includes a gallery tour with making art, and it is said to last around an hour and a half. It is also offered in Spanish. For information or to book tours and programs, call 617-369-3189 or email access@mfa.org.

ISG Museum has volunteers trained to help people with access needs in their groups. These volunteers wear "Ask Me" buttons and can tell you about different facets of the museum. Visitor services and security staff will also know about accessible resources in the museum if you have particular needs. The museum offers tours and programs for mixed school groups, including supporters. Call 617 278 5147.

Boston NHP organizes talks and Park Ranger–led tours for groups and can accommodate people with different access needs and their supporters if they are told beforehand. I'd advise contacting the site at least a month before you plan to visit to book a tour or program and for more information. Call

617 242 5689. School groups can also be hosted with enough notice, although I'd advise even more notice if you want to plan an educational visit.

Visitors with mobility issues at the **Boch Center** can arrange for companion seating next to or near their accessible seats. I'd advise you contact the box office at least a month, a lot longer for popular shows, before you visit to arrange this seating.

Chapter Eight

Chicago, Illinois

On the western shores of Lake Michigan, Chicago—also known as the Windy City—is by far the largest city in the Midwest. Officially, the city spreads into its suburbs in Cook County, with a population of almost 2,900,000. However, the city now merges into other areas and neighboring suburbs for just under 230 square miles with a population of almost 9.5 million. Given this size, the city itself is also a cultural and academic powerhouse, with the University of Chicago and Art Institute of Chicago. This forms the US's third-largest urban area. Before the city was founded, there were several small settlements, including single houses, of Native Americans and people from France and the West Indies[1] on what is now the Chicago River. The first major settlement in Chicago was a fort founded in 1803, with houses being built around in the following decades. This led to the founding of the municipal government of the city in 1837.[2]

INSIDER TIP

Coming from New York, I was surprised to discover that in Chicago there are far more accessible and inclusive theaters than museums. . . . Chicago's theater scene is in many ways more accessible (in many senses of the word, not just in terms of disabilities) than other cities'. . . .

Many of Chicago's storefront theaters are scrappy, experimental and have an emphasis on diversity, equity and inclusion in many senses. Adding accessibility for guests with disabilities into the mix is a natural fit—these theaters' budgets are not large, but they find a way to own their challenges (and commit to improvement) and make accessibility work creatively in their space. This is thanks to . . . resources like CCAC's Accessible Equipment Loan Program.

For theaters I'd suggest places like [these]:

1. Steppenwolf Theatre Company—consistent dedication to access and inclusion
2. Chicago Shakespeare Theater—strong customer service with the front of house staff
3. Lifeline Theatre—a storefront theater in a northern Chicago neighborhood that provides sensory-friendly performances and many other access services
4. Chimera Ensemble—a young theater ensemble that has committed to provide open captioning at every performance

Going to the theater in Chicago is a terrific way to experience accessibility first-hand!

Chicago Cultural Accessibility Consortium (CCAC) offers an Access Calendar that lists all accessible cultural events happening in the Chicago region by date . . .

The Chicago region is striving to become more accessible and inclusive of all visitors each day. Compared to 10 years ago, Chicago's cultural spaces have become increasingly accessible. I encourage any travelers with disabilities visiting Chicago to reach out directly with the organizations to share about your visit and what your needs are. There are more and more options available each year, and not everything is publicized on websites yet.

—Personal communication from Christena Gunther, Founder and Co-Chair of Chicago Cultural Accessibility Consortium, October 2019

The six accessible sites chosen for your Chicago tour are as follows:

The Art Institute of Chicago (ARTIC)

111 South Michigan Ave
Chicago, IL 60603-6404
Tel: 312 443 3600

Where Michigan Avenue meets Adams Street, ARTIC has almost 300,000 artworks, a neoclassical façade, Grecian roof and columns, two lions at its front door, and galleries that have featured in movies such as *Ferris Bueller's Day Off*. Its collections come from diverse international artistic traditions and are gathered with the purpose of education at its heart. The institute was founded in 1879 as part of the rebuilding of the city. Like Boston MFA in the previous chapter, it was founded as both a museum and a school and moved to its current building in 1893. Since this move, the institute has expanded rapidly. Its research library was constructed in 1901 and its modern wing opened in 2009.

The Field Museum (The Field)

1400 South Lake Shore Dr
Chicago, IL 60605

Tel: 312 922 9410
TTY: 312 665 7669

The Field acts as a natural history and anthropology museum, with a collection of almost forty million natural and anthropological pieces and specimens that has grown significantly over its almost one-hundred-year history. It sees its role not only to display and exhibit its pieces. It also develops research projects; forwards knowledge on the natural world; conserves endangered species, the environment, and cultures; and trains new natural scientists. On this latter role, the museum also co-curates exhibitions with Native American communities. The museum is named after Marshall Field, who donated one million dollars to begin its collection in 1893, with the museum itself opening in 1894. After this early museum and collection's steady growth, the museum moved to a site on Lake Michigan's shore in 1921.

Museum of Contemporary Art (MCA)

220 E Chicago Ave
Chicago, IL 60611
Tel: 312 280 2660

With around 45,000 square feet of public spaces and around two thousand artworks in its permanent collection, MCA has what it describes as provocative, experimental artworks, performances, and mature exhibitions. The museum includes touring and special exhibitions, its own exhibitions and art retrospectives, and studies on some of the most important contemporary artwork and artists. It also has a three-hundred-seat theater, studio spaces and spaces for symposia and performances, and a modern library with eighteen thousand documents and a sculpture garden. The museum itself was founded in 1967 without any of its current collection, which was only begun in 1974. It moved to its current buildings in 1996.

Museum of Science and Industry, Chicago (Science and Industry)

5700 South Lake Shore Dr
Chicago, IL 60637
Tel: 773 684 1414
TTY: 773 753 1351

Science and Industry is based on a site of around fourteen acres. Like other museums in this chapter, it has hands-on exhibits, has a largely educational focus, conducts its own research, and trains many of its own scientists. The pieces and specimens in its collections are diverse, with pieces including entire World War II submarines and airplanes from military and domestic fleets as well as small specimens from the natural world. The museum also features educational films in its resident movie theater and regular tours and events. The museum opened in 1933 as part of the city's Century of Progress International Exposition in a building from the Columbian Exposition in 1893. Since these beginnings, it says it has hosted more than 180,000,000 visitors.

The Chicago Theatre (The Chicago)

175 N State St
Chicago, IL 60601
Tel: 888 609 7599

The Chicago stages a diverse range of shows, with plays, magic shows, comedies, speeches, sporting events, popular music concerts, and Broadway and London West End touring shows. Even though it's a commercial theater and a subsidiary of The John Gore Organization, it's based in an elegant building that is worth a visit on its own and a part of "Broadway across America." The theater, which was built in 1921, was originally known as the Balaban and Katz Chicago Theatre. It was added to the National Register of Historic Places in 1979 and listed as a Chicago Landmark in 1983.

Cadillac Palace Theatre (Cadillac Palace)

151 W Randolph St
Chicago, IL 60603
Tel: 312 977 1700

Cadillac Palace shows mostly Broadway shows and has a seating capacity of more than two thousand visitors. It is run and operated by Broadway in Chicago, which also develops pre-Broadway tours and premieres nationwide. The theater was founded as the New Palace Theatre, opening in 1926. It cost around twelve million dollars to build, which was a fortune at the time, and included sumptuous interiors of brass, guilt, and plush seating. During the Second World War, however, this interior was largely painted white to hide its brass, which was needed by the US government for armaments. It was restored to this original state and renamed the Bismarck Theatre in 1984, and then renamed again the Cadillac Palace in 1999.

ACCESS FOR VISITORS WITH SIGHT LOSS

ARTIC has large-print descriptions and Braille texts that can be asked for in advance and free borrowable audio guides at its audio guide desk when you arrive. Call 312 857 7641 or email access@artic.edu. It also has accessible information for visitors with vision loss on its Official Art Institute of Chicago mobile app, which can be used by iOS and Android devices. The app works with Apple's VoiceOver and Android's TalkBack accessible functions and features maps of the museum, its collection, and "The Verbal Description Tour: The Essentials." This last feature provides verbal imaging of artworks. The museum also has free personalized verbally described tours of parts of the museum's collections by specialists and a touch gallery and kits with what it calls TacTiles, each with small relief tiles of artworks. These should all be requested, I'd advise, at least two weeks before you plan to visit.

The Field has a "Field for All" app for Apple and Android devices with accessible information on its exhibitions. It also has bookable tours for visitors with vision loss with verbal imaging and touch objects. These need to be booked before you visit, I'd advise at least a month before. Email mbloom@fieldmuseum.org or call 312 665 7505. The email is linked to an officer at the museum, so I'd check this has not changed before you book.

MCA's website has the Coyote Project, an initiative that provides descriptions of artworks in both short and long forms. The museum's website has audio description and is largely accessible to visitors with vision loss. I'd advise contacting the museum at least two weeks before your visit. Email BoxOffice@mcachicago.org.

Science and Industry has sighted guides for tours and can offer visitors visual assistance in the stores and food court.

Cadillac Palace has audio-described shows. I'd advise contacting the theater at least a month before you plan to visit for details. Call 312 977 1700 and press 5 or TTY: 800 359 2525.

ACCESS FOR VISITORS WITH HEARING LOSS

ARTIC's auditoria have borrowable assistive listening systems from staff for a number of its tours, which can be requested when you book the tour. It also has hearing loops that are compatible with adapted hearing aids in its auditoria. The museum has an app for Apple and Android devices with information about the artworks through its *Look It Up* function. The museum runs ASL tours that you'll need to book at least a month in advance. Call 312 443 3680 or email access@artic.edu.

The Field has a "Field for All" app, with written information on its exhibitions and information on visit schedules. This app is available from Apple and Android stores, and details of this app are available on the museum website.

MCA has captions and borrowable assistive listening devices for a number of tours, shows, educational programs, and talks in the museum's theater.

The museum also has ASL tours. I'd advise contacting the museum at least two weeks before you plan to visit for more information. Call 312 397 4010 or email BoxOffice@mcachicago.org.

Science and Industry has ASL interpreters for tours, plus scripts for tours, films in its theater, and educational programs. I'd advise contacting the museum at least two weeks before you plan to visit. Call 773 684 1414 or TTY: 773 753 1351.

The Chicago has free borrowable assistive listening devices at the coat check; you'll need to leave official photo ID with the theater until you return the device. The theater also has ASL interpretation for a number of shows. I'd advise contacting the theater at least a month before you visit for information and to book. Email disabledservices@msg.com or call 888 609 7599.

Cadillac Palace has free borrowable assisted listening devices from the house manager. I'd advise you to get to the theater at least half an hour before your show, and you'll need to leave official photo ID until you return the device. The theater also has ASL-interpreted shows and shows with captions advertised on its calendar and website, although I'd advise you to contact the theater at least a month before you visit for information. Call 312 977 1700 extension 5 or TTY: 800 359 2525, or email accessibility@broadwayinchicago.com.

ACCESS FOR VISITORS WITH LEARNING DISABILITIES, MEMORY LOSS, AND AUTISM HIGHER ON THE SPECTRUM

ARTIC has a number of programs for people with memory loss and learning disabilities. For instance, its Art in the Moment program is designed for visitors with dementia and those who care for them. The program offers work in small groups, discussions, and art exercises with art therapists. I'd advise that you contact the museum at least a month before you plan to visit for information and to book. Call 312 443 3680 or email access@artic.edu. The museum also has social stories and a family room for visitors with autism higher on the spectrum. Again, I'd advise you contact the museum at least two weeks before you visit to arrange these services and for information about its social stories.

The Field's "Field for All" app has information to plan and schedule visits and find suitable exhibits and timings. In addition, the museum has free programs for visitors over eight years old with learning difficulties. For instance, its PlayLab Accessibility Days program has tours for small groups of adults, and its PlayLab Sensory Saturdays program has touch and low-sensory tours for small groups of younger visitors and families. I'd advise that you contact the museum at least a month before you plan to visit for information and to book. Email accessibility@fieldmuseum.org or call 312 665 7695 or TTY: 312 665 7669.

Science and Industry has programs for visitors with learning disabilities. For instance, its Low-Sensory Early Exploration program has sensory-friendly and low-sensory tours of exhibitions with fewer visitors and a quiet space. I'd advise contacting the museum at least a month before you plan to visit for information and to book. Call 773 684 1414 or TTY: 773 753 1351. The museum also has a sensory map and a social narrative/story on its accessibility webpage, which can be downloaded before you visit the museum.

ACCESS FOR VISITORS WITH MOBILITY ISSUES

ARTIC has accessible spaces in its parking garages for automobiles with disability symbols, a valet parking service, accessible entrances with ramps, and a drop-off point close to its main entrance. I'd advise contacting the museum at least a week before you plan to visit for information. Call 312 443 3680 or email access@artic.edu. Inside, the museum has elevator access to all floors and free borrowable wheelchairs at its checkrooms. What's more, for visitors who can't get to the museum, it also provides slides from the collection and discussions about its artworks via telephone to visitors from the US. Call 877 797 7299 (you will have to register as a user), email coviaconnections@covia.org, or visit https://covia.org/services/well-connected/.

The Field can be reached via the local paratransit service, called the Chicago ADA Service, with information about booking on its website (https://www.cookdupagetransportation.com/). It also has accessible spaces in its parking lot and garage for automobiles with disability symbols, although these spaces charge for parking. Inside, the museum has elevators to all public floors, its bathrooms are mostly accessible, and it has borrowable wheelchairs at its east and south entrances and coat check.

MCA's parking garage has accessible parking spaces for automobiles with disability symbols—although the museum states you'll need to validate this parking at its admissions desk or coat check. Inside, it has elevator access to all floors, although one elevator has restricted access. I'd advise checking with staff during your visit about this access. The museum's store, theater, restaurant, and bar have largely accessible entrances, its terrace has automatic doors and a ramp, and its bathrooms are largely accessible. The museum also has free borrowable wheelchairs at its coat check and accessible seating and spaces in its theater. I'd advise contacting the museum for information about your specific access needs before you visit; call 312 397 4010.

Science and Industry has accessible parking spaces in its underground parking (for large automobiles) and its parking garage (for more regular automobiles) for automobiles with disability symbols—the garage also has an elevator. The museum's main entrance has a push-button door, and its bathrooms are largely accessible. The museum has elevators and ramps to all floors in the museum, and its theater has accessible and companion seats and access via elevator. I'd advise contacting the museum before you plan to visit for information. Call 773 684 1414 or TTY: 773 753 1351.

If you have mobility issues, **The Chicago** advises arriving at least one hour before your show starts, through the main entrance to give you time to get around the building and to your seats. It has elevators as well as accessible and companion seating in its auditorium at different prices. I'd advise you contact the theater at least a month before you visit for information and to ask about booking. Their box office number is 888 609 7599 or TTY: 711 (this number takes you to the relay center; from there ask for the theater).

Cadillac Palace has accessible seats with different prices, and it is also possible to book adjoining or nearby companion seats. I'd advise you contact the theater at least a month before you plan to visit for information and to book seats. Call 312 977 1700, extension 5, TTY: 800 359 2525, or email accessibility@broadwayinchicago.com. The theater also has elevator access for visitors with mobility issues, and its bathrooms, concession stands, and water fountains are mostly accessible.

ACCESS FOR SUPPORTERS

ARTIC's programs for visitors with access needs can also be attended by supporters, friends, and families, with their Art in the Moment program also giving space for caregivers to visit and talk to others in the same position. I'd advise contacting the museum at least a month before you plan to visit for information and booking. Call 312 443 3680 or email access@artic.edu.

The Field advertises officers and guest relations associates can support visitors with access needs in the museum. I'd advise contacting the museum at least a week before you plan to visit for information about this service. Email accessibility@fieldmuseum.org or call 312 922 9410 and request the access department or TTY: 312 665 7669. In addition, if you have access needs and visit or attend programs for visitors with learning difficulties with a professional supporter who is providing care, the supporter *may* be entitled to a free ticket. Again, contact the museum for information and conditions for these tickets.

If you have mobility issues and are visiting **The Chicago**, it may be possible to book extra companion seats next to the access space. The theater states that it can also provide support from staff for visitors with vision or hearing loss who want to visit independently. I'd advise contacting the theater before you plan to visit for information and to arrange support.

Cadillac Palace offers extra seats for friends and supporters at the same price next to or near visitors with mobility issues. To book accessible seats, I'd advise contacting the theater at least a month before you plan to visit for information. Call 312 341 2389 or email accessibility@broadwayinchicago.com.

Chapter Nine

Denver, Colorado

My first memory of Denver is leaning my head out of a train window in the middle of January and thinking how fresh—and cold—the air was. The Mile High City, so-called because it's 5,280 feet above sea level, is one of the highest cities in the US. The city sits at the feet of the Rocky Mountains, which form a spine down the West of the US, running from north to south down its body. It also sits southeast of the Rocky Mountains National Park, and its northern border wraps around the Rocky Mountain Arsenal National Park. To put it another way, if you want to see views of spectacular mountains, this is the city to visit. The city itself was founded in 1858 on the banks of the River Platte, and named after James W. Denver, an early governor of the territory.

INSIDER TIP

The Denver Art Museum . . . has programs [which are] accessible by calling in advance. They have put a lot of effort into their accessibility programming and are planning on adding major features in their new space by designing in access in the renovations that are taking place right now. [These are to be completed soon] . . .

Founded in 1989, Phamaly Theatre Company was created when five students from the Boettcher School in Denver, all living with disabilities, grew frustrated with the lack of theatrical opportunities for people living with disabilities. The group decided to create a theater company that would provide individuals with disabilities the opportunity to perform. Also, Denver Center for the Preforming Arts and Arvada Center [provide good accessible performances] . . .

[For access to non-artistic cultural places,] check out a new interior navigation system they have just installed [at Denver Museum of Nature and

Science]. They too have quite a few accessible features if you are interested in that type of museum.

—Ann Cunningham, artist and educator, personal correspondence,
September 2019

The five accessible sites chosen for your Denver tour are the following:

Denver Art Museum (DAM)

100 W 14th Avenue Pkwy
Denver, CO 80204
Tel: 720 913 0074 or 720 865 5000

DAM is around 350,000 square feet, with a collection of more than seventy thousand artworks in twelve permanent collections. These collections are largely themed geographically, and include Asian, European and American, African, American Indian, Spanish Colonial, Oceanic, pre-Columbian, and Western American artworks, architecture, design, graphics, modern and contemporary art, photography, and textiles. The collection was founded in 1893 by the Denver Artists' Club, and its first museum opened in 1949 on 14th Avenue Parkway. In the 1950s, a center for children's art activities was added, and in 1971 its north building was added. In the new millennium, the museum went through further expansion, when in 2006 new galleries, three temporary exhibition spaces, and art storage were added. This was followed in 2014 when its library was added.

Molly Brown House (Molly Brown's)

1340 Pennsylvania St
Denver, CO 80203
Tel: 303 832 4092

Molly Brown's is locally nicknamed the House of Lions because of the lion statues at its entrance, although the house is officially named after the former owner, Margaret "Molly" Brown. Molly was a *Titanic* survivor, known as the Unsinkable Molly Brown, who bought the house in 1894 with her husband. Molly died in 1932 and the house was sold, losing its status as a family home after changing hands several times and becoming run down. The house reached its lowest point as a boarding house from 1958 until it was bought with the plan of renovating it as a symbol of early Denver. In 1970, what is now the museum was founded as Historic Denver, Inc., and much effort was put into the renovations that brought the house back to its original grandeur. At the time of writing, the museum was undergoing major renovations and was scheduled to reopen in May 2020. However, following the coronavirus lockdown of 2020, it is unknown when this will now be.

Denver Museum of Nature & Science (Nature & Science)

2001 Colorado Blvd
Denver, CO 80205
Tel: 303 370 6000

Nature & Science is an independent, not-for-profit Smithsonian Institution affiliate founded to develop the academic culture of Denver. It is more than 715,000 square feet, with collections totaling over a million anthropological pieces and pieces from nature in collections, an archive, and a library. It also incorporates academic research and educational programs. Nature & Science was founded in 1900 and opened to the public in 1908 as a traditional natural history museum. It expanded quickly, and in 1918 a further wing was added to its building to accommodate its growing collections. In 1948, the museum went through a further evolution and was renamed the Denver Museum of Natural History, and in 2000 it was renamed again the Denver Museum of Nature & Science. Since 1988, the museum has been largely funded by Scientific and Cultural Facilities District (SCFD) and public donors.

Children's Museum of Denver (Children's Museum)

2121 Children's Museum Dr
Denver, CO 80211
Tel: 303 433 7444

Children's Museum is a not-for-profit organization and the city's first children's museum, which was designed to educate and stimulate children's imaginations through interactive, exciting exhibitions. The museum opened in a converted school bus in 1973 and expanded rapidly. Shortly afterward, it moved to a building on Bannock Street in the city, and in 1984 it moved to a purpose-built site bordering the Platte River. Over the following four decades, the museum's visitor figures rose to the hundreds of thousands and, reflecting its evolving institution, in 2015 it moved to its current nine-acre campus.

Denver Center for the Performing Arts (The Center)

1101 13th St
Denver, CO 80204
Tel: 303 893 4000

The Center is based on a large, modernist campus for the performing arts, and has a number of performance spaces. It stages shows as diverse as Broadway musicals to plays written and staged by its own DCPA theater company. Its spaces include a number of theaters and an opera house, and it is the site of the original Denver Municipal Auditorium, which opened in 1908. Its original charter began in the 1950s as the Bonfils Theatre, Colfax Avenue, which was an amateur community theater company that became the old Bonfils Theatre, then the Denver Center, during the 1960s. Its first large theater then opened on its current site in 1978.

ACCESS FOR VISITORS WITH SIGHT LOSS

DAM has large-print and Braille documents for a number of its special exhibitions and audio guides for regular visits to the museum. To get access to these documents and devices, ask staff at the museum for information when you first visit. The museum also runs programs for visitors with sight loss, and access tours can be arranged for individuals or small groups if requested. For example, its Tactile Tour program includes touch and the verbal imaging of pieces during tours of selected artworks. I'd advise contacting the museum at least two weeks before you plan to visit for information and to book this and similar tours. Email access@denverartmuseum.org or call 720 913 0074. The museum also has tactile tables, with multisensory objects for all its visitors. These are put in a different gallery every month.

    Nature & Science has information in Braille around the museum, including its elevators, and borrowable Braille maps at its main information desk. The museum also has standard tours, during which a number of pieces are touchable, including a Navajo hogan, mineral specimens, large models of butterflies, sheep horns, skulls, bison fur, tracks, scats, antler velvet, jaws, and the teeth and cushioned hooves of a bighorn sheep. I'd advise contacting the museum at least a month before you plan to visit for information and to book these tours. Call 303 370 6000.

    It can be said that **Children's Museum**'s regular exhibits and pieces are meant to be touched by all users, so they are automatically more accessible to people with low vision. The museum also has a limited amount of materials in accessible formats that you can download from its website or get from the museum's front desk. If you have specific needs not identified by the museum's regular accessible service, you can contact the museum in advance about special accommodations, I'd advise at least two weeks before you plan to visit.

    The Center has audio description for a number of its shows, available with at least two weeks' notice before you plan to visit. You can also book tickets for shows on specified dates marked with the code AUDIO on their website, although I'd advise contacting the site before you plan to visit for more information about these performances. The Center also offers visitors large-print programs through its ushers and borrowable Braille programs via its access services. You'll need to ask for these Braille documents to be made at least two weeks before you plan to visit.

ACCESS FOR VISITORS WITH HEARING LOSS

DAM has captions on a number of its regular videos in some of its special exhibitions, and scripts for these videos are made available through members of staff when you visit the museum. The museum also offers tours for people with hearing loss and, for example, ASL interpreters can be arranged for individuals or small groups. I'd advise contacting the museum at least a month before you plan to visit for information and to request an ASL interpreter and tour. Email access@denverartmuseum.org or call 720 913 0074.

Tours at **Molly Brown's** may be able to offer assistive listening devices on the day and scripts in English, French, and Spanish if you contact the venue beforehand. The museum also offers to arrange ASL interpreters for tours, although you'll need to contact the museum at least two weeks before you plan to visit. Call 303 832 4092 extension 17 or email access@mollybrown.org.

Nature & Science has captions on a number of its videos and has borrowable caption devices and assisted listening devices in its IMAX theater from its ushers or box office. You'll need to arrive at least twenty minutes before the start of the IMAX show to arrange for these devices, and you'll need to leave official photo ID until you return your device. The museum's planetarium also has assisted listening devices from its staff, and again they ask you to arrive early (at least half an hour before the show) to arrange for a device. In addition, the museum's guest services can arrange free ASL interpreters for its regular programs and lectures. I'd advise contacting them at least a month before you plan to visit the museum. Call 303 370 6000 or email guestservices@dmns.org.

Children's Museum has accessible exhibition materials as text available before you visit, which you can download from its website or get from its front desk. In addition, similar to its appeal to children with vision loss, the regular interactive nature of the exhibits can make the museum more accessible to children with hearing loss.

The Center has borrowable caption and assisted listening devices for a number of its shows that you can get from ushers. I'd advise arriving at least half an hour before your show to ask about a device. You can find shows with captions on its calendar and website advertised with the symbol OCAP, and I'd advise contacting The Center for information about finding and booking captioned performances. The Center also offers shows with ASL interpretation, which are advertised on its calendar and website using the code ASL. Again, I'd contact The Center at least a month before you plan to visit for information about booking seating near the interpreter, or look on the website for information about booking these shows online using codes. Call 303 893 4000.

ACCESS FOR VISITORS WITH LEARNING DISABILITIES, MEMORY LOSS, AND AUTISM HIGHER ON THE SPECTRUM

DAM has programs for visitors with memory loss and learning difficulties. For instance, Art & About Tours is for visitors with Alzheimer's or dementia and their caregivers or supporters. Each tour has a different theme and includes interaction with and conversation about the artworks. Email access@denverartmuseum.org or call 720 913 0074. The museum also has programs and tours for visitors with autism higher on the spectrum and others who need lower sensory stimulation. This program involves tours when the museum is quiet, and it offers sensory-reducing equipment, a quiet space, and art making—although the latter is optional. In addition, the museum offers bespoke access tours for individuals or small groups with learning disabilities or memory loss. I'd advise getting in touch with the museum at least a month before you plan to visit for information and to arrange a tour.

The museum also offers social stories along with SPARK explorer packs with low-sensory tools. These can all be arranged in advance for visitors with autism higher on the spectrum and their families. I'd advise contacting the museum at least a week before you plan to visit for information on tours and to ask for a pack to be made available. Call 720 913 0074 or email access@denverartmuseum.org.

Molly Brown's also has a number of programs for people with learning difficulties and memory loss. For instance, its SPARK! programs are for visitors with memory loss, such as early stage dementia, that are designed with memory-stimulating tours and can be attended with family, friends, or supporters. At the time of writing, the house is also about to begin a series of sensory-friendly mornings for families that have members with autism higher on the spectrum. I'd contact the museum to find out more and see its calendar for information. The museum also has downloadable social stories in English and Spanish on its website for visitors with autism higher on the spectrum and learning difficulties.

Nature & Science has borrowable wiggle cushions and noise-reducing headphones at its information desk for visitors with autism higher on the spectrum and others sensitive to noise and sensory stimulation.

The Children's Museum has a schedule board, which is a simplified scheme of the museum that allows you to plan your visit. The museum also offers a guide called "How We Play Museum Guide" for visitors with learning disabilities and their families. The guide has pictures and simple language that describes ways to engage with exhibits. It also organizes a morning tour that only a small number of visitors attend, with reduced background noise for children with autism higher on the spectrum and learning disabilities. I'd advise contacting the museum at least a month before you plan to visit for more information and to book. Call 303 561 0108. In addition, the museum has a Center for the Young Child to stimulate young children's senses, particularly those with learning disabilities. Members of staff at the museum can tell you where this is.

The Center has sensory-friendly services for visitors with autism higher on the spectrum. Ask staff for information about these services when you visit for your show.

ACCESS FOR VISITORS WITH MOBILITY ISSUES

DAM has accessible parking on 13th Avenue and on the second level of the nearby cultural center parking garage for automobiles with disability symbols. The museum's main entrance also has automatic doors. Inside, the museum states that its public areas are accessible to visitors with mobility issues, with largely accessible bathrooms available. The museum also has free borrowable wheelchairs, although you'll need to leave official photo ID until they are returned. For more information, contact the museum before you visit. Email access@denverartmuseum.org.

Molly Brown's has accessible parking spaces outside; check with the museum for more information. The house also has information and images about its rooms on its upper floors for visitors who can't reach them and an accessible bathroom with a disability lift to get to it.

Nature & Science has accessible parking spaces in its main parking lot and underground parking garage, plus push-button doors at its main entrance. Inside, the museum has elevators to most of its public areas, including its IMAX theater and accessible bathrooms. Ask staff for their locations. The museum also has free borrowable canes and wheelchairs at its information desk.

The Center has accessible parking spaces in its parking garage for automobiles with disability symbols and a drop-off area close to its building on 14th Street. Inside, The Center has borrowable wheelchairs and accessible seating for visitors with mobility issues in all its theaters, with seating for companions next to or near these. I'd advise you to contact The Center at least a month before you plan to visit for information about booking the seats and wheelchairs. The Center also states that its tours are accessible for visitors with mobility issues as they have ramps, elevators, and a disability lift inside the building.

Chapter 9

ACCESS FOR SUPPORTERS

DAM organizes tours for small groups including people with access needs. You'll need to contact the museum at least two weeks before you plan to visit for information and to book. In addition, the museum's Art & About Tours for visitors with dementia allow caregivers or supporters to attend too. Email access@denverartmuseum.org or call 720 913 0074.

Molly Brown's is to begin sensory-friendly mornings for families that have members with autism higher on the spectrum. I'd advise contacting the museum for information. In addition, the museum offers more established SPARK! programs for visitors with memory loss, such as early stage dementia, with their family, friends, or supporters.

Nature & Science offers a single professional caregiver free entry to the museum and its IMAX theater and planetarium if he or she is supporting the visitor when he or she attends. The caregiver must be booked through guest services when he or she attends to get a free ticket. I'd advise contacting the museum before you plan to visit for information by calling 303 370 6000.

Children's Museum also offers a morning for visitors with sensory sensitivities and their families and friends or caregivers. I'd advise you to contact the museum before you plan to visit for information and to book. Call 303 561 0108.

Chapter Ten

Houston, Texas

Named after General Sam Houston, an early president of Texas, Houston was founded in 1836 on land bought by two brothers. The oldest and original parts of the city are based on land near Buffalo Bayou, and the whole modern city is just inland from Galveston and Trinity bays, off the Gulf of Mexico. Houston is the largest city by population in the southern states of the US and has an ethnically diverse population, which makes for interesting restaurants in its urban area. The city also has a very modern center surrounded by almost symmetric suburbs, with wide roads. Its downtown is filled with tall glass, steel, and often mirrored skyscrapers. It is well known for its business and space sciences and is also an airline hub to South and Central America and beyond.

INSIDER TIP

Like other cities in this book, Houston is very warm in the summer and, being close to the Gulf of Mexico, can be prone to tropical storms—these storms can be spectacular but, like Florida over the gulf, it's best to be inside when they hit. This means that if you're a fan of outdoor heat and outdoor living, this is a wonderful city to be out in during spring, winter, and fall mornings and becomes a particularly interesting place to be out at night.

Houston is not like the regular image of Texas. Sure, you can see the odd cowboy around the town, but it's also a cosmopolitan city with an urban atmosphere and a love of culture—often not just its own but the culture of others too.

However, what Houston is perhaps best known for in the wider world is its space program. Even though the National Aeronautics and Space Administration (NASA) launch pads are outside the city, you'll see evidence of its influence all over town, from the souvenirs in the airport shops to the Space Center Houston in town. It would be a real shame to make it to Houston and not visit this center, especially as it's a Smithsonian venue with real rockets and memorabilia from the heyday of space exploration.

The six accessible sites chosen for your Houston tour are as follows:

The Museum of Fine Arts, Houston (MFA Houston)

1001 Bissonnet St
Houston, TX 77005
Tel: 713 639 7300

MFA Houston has artworks and design pieces dating from antiquity until the present, and is based in the newly opened Brown Foundation, Inc. Plaza, which as I write is less than a year old. Its collections are mostly encyclopedic and are often developed according to type of artwork and historical period. These collections include its Bayou Bend Collection of American artworks and its American and European collection of decorative arts. The museum also houses the International Center for the Arts of the Americas (ICAA), a research institute for contemporary Latin American art, a cinema, and libraries. MFA Houston was founded in 1900 and opened in 1910. Its original building was the first art museum in the state. Since this period, it has gone through a long period of expansion: it opened its Caroline Wiess Law Building, extensions in 1958 and 1974; its Lillie and Hugh Roy Cullen Sculpture Garden opened in 1986; its Audrey Jones Beck Building opened in 2000; the Glassell School of Art in 2018; and its last phase of development at the time of writing, its plaza, opened in 2018.

The Houston Museum of Natural Science (Houston MNS)

5555 Hermann Park Dr
Houston, TX 77030
Tel: 713 639 4629

Houston MNS has a significant collection of pieces from biology, the earth, and the cosmos, plus a small collection of living creatures and anthropological pieces largely reflecting Native American culture. These pieces are featured in permanent and temporary exhibitions on astronomy and space science, Native American culture, fossils, geology, the nature of chemicals, and local wildlife. The museum also has a planetarium, a giant screen movie theater, and a butterfly center. The museum hosts more than half a million school children per year through school trips and outreach, and it is said to be a major resource for local schools and curricula. Houston MNS was founded in 1909 as the Houston Museum and Scientific Society, and after sixty years of expansion its current building opened in 1969.

The Space Center Houston (Space Center)

1601 NASA Parkway
Houston, TX 77058
Tel: 281 244 2100

The Space Center was established by the National Aeronautics and Space Administration (NASA) and highlights all aspects of Houston's most famous asset: its place as the launch site for America's best-known space missions. Based in a building of approximately a quarter of a million square feet, the center was designed to narrate NASA's space program and to educate its visitors about the nature of space flight, discovery, science, and engineering. It has original pieces from space missions and multimedia and interactive exhibitions, and it all tells the story of the history of space exploration. The center hosts the Manned Space Flight Education Foundation, a not-for-profit educational foundation with a space museum and education programs largely for children. It also houses the Official Visitor Center of NASA Johnson Space Center. The whole center has just over one million visitors a year. Space Center opened in 1992 and is now an affiliate of the Smithsonian Institute.

The Children's Museum of Houston (Children's Museum)

1500 Binz St
Houston, TX 77004-7112
Tel: 713 522 1138

Children's Museum is focused on child-centered learning, including interactive exhibitions and learning zones featuring issues that have an impact on modern children. Its zones include an auditorium, a Tot Spot, FlowWorks, Kidtropolis, USA, PowerPlay, CYBERCHASE, How Does It Work?, Invention Convention, EcoStation, and a Building Zone. It can also offer bespoke learning and support for parents' home-learning. Importantly, the museum provides special learning opportunities to children with physical and learning access needs. The museum's attendance is generally just under 800,000 visitors a year, with just short of a third of these visits being visitors with free entry, a large number of which are low-income families. Children's Museum opened in 1984 as a not-for-profit organization.

Hobby Center (The Hobby)

800 Bagby St, Ste. 300

Houston, TX 77002
Tel: 713 315 2400

The Hobby has two venues organized and run by the The Hobby Center Foundation: the Sarofim Hall, which has a seating capacity of around 2,650, and Zilkha Hall, which has a seating capacity of around 500. Its foundation is a not-for-profit organization, largely funded by businesses in the local area and private donations, as well as ticket sales. The center stages plays, musicals, and contemporary and traditional music shows among other performances, and it often tries to represent the diversity of the local Texan population by promoting local arts groups in its programming. In addition, it has resident performance companies that develop and run series of their own shows, including a Broadway at the Hobby Center and Theatre Under the Stars. It also organizes education and community engagement programs. The Hobby opened in 2002 in the Houston Theater District.

Alley Theatre (The Alley)

615 Texas Ave
Houston, TX 77002
Tel: 713 220 5700

The Alley is a modern, not-for-profit arts center comprising two main theaters: Hubbard Theatre, which has seating for 774, and the Neuhaus Theatre, which has a seating capacity of 296. It largely stages plays by Houston-based and touring theatrical companies, including those by its resident theatrical company, and runs educational programs and outreach—the latter two include talks about its shows and workshops with actors. It states that it stages around five hundred performances in each theater per season, and its theaters and educational programs combined have around 200,000 visitors per year. The Alley was established in the 1940s by a local drama teacher, and its first performance was 1947. The first of its resident theaters opened in 1968 in its now distinctive modernist building.

ACCESS FOR VISITORS WITH SIGHT LOSS

MFA Houston's main site runs a program, Art Beyond Sight, for visitors with sight loss. The program has verbal imaging and the opportunity to touch featured artworks. At the time of writing, it's available on regular Saturdays and is free, although I recommend you book at least a month in advance. Email tours@mfah.org or call 713 639 7300.

Houston MNS has an app that can be used on Android and Apple devices. It has accessible information that can be downloaded before you visit its museum. They also offer large-print labels to download before your visit on PDF for the Hall of Paleontology, although more are to arrive soon for other galleries—being PDFs, these will have limited access to screen readers. In addition, the museum also has irregular touch tours for visitors with vision loss that can be booked before you visit. I'd recommend you call them at least a month before you plan to visit. Email accessprogramming@hmns.org or call 713 639 4620. The tours include verbal imaging and touch objects.

Space Center also has an app with an interactive map and guide that is largely accessible to people with vision loss—although the map is less accessible to visitors with no sight. It is recommended you download it before going to the museum in order to plan your museum visit and route.

Children's Museum has regular interactive, multimedia, and hands-on activities that are relatively more accessible to visitors with vision loss. The museum also has iPads with Museum Discovery Guides, which are also largely accessible to most users with vision loss, and Braille signs throughout the museum, such as on doors and in bathrooms, entrances, and elevators.

The Hobby has borrowable large-print and Braille programs and playbills, which are held by members of staff when you visit before your show. I'd advise arriving in plenty of time and contacting the center at least two weeks before you visit to make sure the document you want can be made available on the night. Call 713 315 2412 or email access@thehobbycenter.org. The center also arranges audio description for some of its shows, which have extra descriptions of sets, designs, and so forth. These are advertised on its calendar or through contacting them directly. During these shows, the center has borrowable devices that receive descriptions; you'll have to leave official photo ID until these devices are returned. Again, contact the center at least two weeks before you visit to get further information about the shows and how you pick up a device.

ACCESS FOR VISITORS WITH HEARING LOSS

MFA Houston has borrowable assisted listening devices and assistive caption devices for shows in its theater. Note that listening devices are for all shows, lectures, and films, but the caption devices are only for digital films. These devices are available from staff members in the auditorium when you visit. I'd advise getting there at least half an hour early to arrange for them.

Houston MNS has a downloadable app for Android and Apple, with written information about exhibitions that can be used as you tour the museum. A number of films running in the museum's giant screen theater have captions, which run on a small borrowable device. To arrange for a device when you arrive and for more information, please tell the museum when you book your theater ticket. Email accessprogramming@hmns.org or call 713 639 4620.

Space Center also has a downloadable app for Apple and Android devices with interactive maps and guides that is largely accessible through text and images. The center's attraction, the Mission Briefing Center, has an induction loop for visitors with adapted hearing aids. It also has closed captions on numerous visual displays throughout the site.

Children's Museum has regular interactive exhibitions with text and multimedia elements that are often more easily understood by people with hearing loss. The museum also has television screens around its spaces with information.

The Hobby has captions displayed near its stage for numerous shows and shows with ASL interpretation. Information about these is generally advertised on its calendar, and the center advises that you contact them directly when you book your ticket to ask for a reserved seat near these captions or in view of the signer. Call 713 315 2412 or email access@thehobbycenter.org. The center also has borrowable assisted listening devices, so contact the center at least two weeks beforehand so they can organize a device for when you arrive.

The Alley has free assisted listening devices for shows in its auditoria that can be borrowed from staff when you get to the center. You'll need to leave official photo ID when you borrow a device, and I'd advise you to contact the theater before you plan to visit for information. Call 713 220 5700. The center's Hubbard Theatre has an induction loop system for visitors with adapted hearing aids and implants. Contact the center before you plan to visit for more information about this system. The center also has captions on a screen overhead for a number of shows, which are advertised in its calendar. The theater advises you to contact its box office when you plan to book your ticket, get information about these shows, explain your access needs, and book a seat near the caption screens.

ACCESS FOR VISITORS WITH LEARNING DISABILITIES, MEMORY LOSS, AND AUTISM HIGHER ON THE SPECTRUM

Houston MNS has borrowable visual vocabulary cards for visitors with learning difficulties, and the museum advises that you contact them to ask about these cards before you plan to visit. Email accessprogramming@hmns.org or call 713 639 4625. The museum also has borrowable sensory backpacks, which can be found at museum services. These packs are sensory-friendly for visitors with autism higher on the spectrum and learning difficulties, and the touch objects in these packs are also useful for people with sight loss. You'll need to leave official photo ID until you bring the pack back. For visitors with autism higher on the spectrum, the museum advises that you call them to ask about better visiting times. Call 713 639 4629.

Space Center's Science and Space Exploration Learning Center is an IBCCES Certified Autism Center. The center holds sensory-friendly events with small group tours that have lower sensory input, and there are sensory backpacks at its guest services desk for those who want to visit independently during regular times. The packs include sensory-reducing devices and informative books for visitors with autism higher on the spectrum. I'd advise contacting the center before you visit for more information on these packs and events. Email accessibility@spacecenter.org.

Children's Museum is also an IBCCES Certified Autism Center. It has sensory-friendly days, which are often on irregular Mondays when the museum is normally closed to the public. These days are focused on children with autism higher on the spectrum, although all children with disabilities can attend. Sensory-friendly days offer visitors smaller-size groups, reduced sound and lighting, increased "visual signage," and borrowable sunglasses and headphones. Before visiting, the museum offers visitors with autism higher on the spectrum and learning disabilities downloadable story books in English and Spanish on its website. These outline ways of visiting the museum and allow you to choose routes.

ACCESS FOR VISITORS WITH MOBILITY ISSUES

MFA Houston states it's accessible to visitors with mobility issues, including its sculpture garden, using your own mobility devices. Outside, it has a drop-off area near its entrance and access spaces in its parking garages for automobiles with disability symbols. Inside, the museum has borrowable wheelchairs at the coat check area and the lobby, and you'll need to leave official photo ID until the chair is returned. It also has seats around the building for those who need to take frequent rests, although I'd advise contacting the museum directly if you have specific mobility requests. Email guestservices@mfah.org or call 713 639 7300.

Houston MNS has an organized drop-off service called METROLift that can get you to the museum. Call 713 225 6716 about this service. The museum also has accessible parking spots available to the front of the museum and its parking garage. Inside, the museum has elevators near the entrance and throughout the museum, plus bathrooms with access for people with mobility issues. The museum also has borrowable wheelchairs for children and adults (few sites do this) at its museum services desk, and ramps can be arranged by security staff from the parking garage. I'd advise contacting the museum at least a week before you visit to arrange this service. Email accessprogramming@hmns.org or call 713 639 4620.

Space Center has accessible parking near the entrance and in the parking lot nearby, although parking is not free in the lot. The center also has NASA trams and buses that often have lifts for those with mobility issues. A number of its bathrooms, its performances, and its Zero-G Diner are largely accessible for people with mobility issues. The center also has borrowable wheelchairs from its guest services. Uniquely, the Space Center does outreach in schools, if you have a child with mobility issues who lives locally. For full access information to and from the center, I'd advise contacting them a week before you plan to visit, or, if you want to arrange outreach, several months in advance. Email accessibility@spacecenter.org or call 281 244 2100.

Children's Museum has accessible spaces in the parking garage with wheelchair ramps in the garage and out front. Inside, the museum also has borrowable wheelchairs at its information booth.

The Hobby has valet parking staff who can help with access from automobiles with disability symbols. I'd advise you to contact the center before you visit to arrange for support as soon as you get there. Call 713 315 2412 or email access@thehobbycenter.org. Inside, the center has wheelchair-accessible seating and staff who can meet you and provide support with mobility when you arrive. You'll need to tell the center your seating and access needs when you book your tickets, so I'd advise calling their box office personally at 800 982 2787 or 713 558 8887. The center also advises that you arrive more than half an hour before your show, as it is easier to get access to the auditoria before other visitors take their seats.

The Alley has an accessible drop-off zone close to its entrance and accessible spaces on some levels of its parking garage for automobiles with disability symbols, with an elevator to get into the center. Inside, the center also has an accessible elevator to its Neuhaus Theatre and accessible seating areas and seats for visitors with mobility issues in both theaters. The center asks that you tell them if you want a parking space or accessible seat when you book your tickets, and I would advise you call the ticket line to explain your access needs. Call 713 220 5700.

ACCESS FOR SUPPORTERS

For information about **MFA Houston**'s accessibility and programs for visitors with disabilities, email tours@mfah.org or call 713 639 7300.

For specialist access and to ask about group tours at **Houston MNS**, email accessprogramming@hmns.org or call 713 639 4620.

Space Center asks parents to let them know if their child has access needs, so they can discuss a way of accessing the center. Email accessibility@spacecenter.org.

Chapter Eleven

Los Angeles, California

Unlike the other cities in this book, when I write about Los Angeles (LA), I'm writing about a county rather than just a city. The city of LA itself is a strange-shaped mixture of suburbs with a modern city center well inland, and the usual concentration of skyscrapers downtown. However, the county of LA is a sprawling mass of smaller, equally famous cities such as Beverly Hills and West Hollywood. This sprawl, the movie and television capital of the US, is squeezed in on two sides by hills and mountains to its eastern inland, and the beaches and Pacific Ocean to its west. Notice that landscape as you land at LAX or arrive by automobile, train, or bus. Feel free to explore the whole of this amazing, wonderful, mixed-up assault on the senses that is sparkle-town.

INSIDER TIP

LA is big. Not just regular big, but really, really big.

It is more of a country in itself than it is a part of the US. It's so different and self-contained and bears so little resemblance to the states that immediately surround it. While you're traveling through it—which will take a long time, by the way—remember that it bears a greater resemblance to Madrid, Shanghai, Mexico City, London, Tokyo, Singapore, Mumbai, or Dubai than it does to the Midwest or the East Coast, or even to most other cities in California. Its temperature can also get very hot. I've visited it when it was so hot that it rivaled Dubai for temperatures. For this reason, I'd adjust your visit according to the season and long-range weather forecast.

Bearing all these things in mind, my tip for LA is to focus on what I feel are local LA icons. Not the LA that the world thinks it sees, nor the bus-tour-star-homes-spotting LA that many tourists are taken to see, but the local culture that people from LA appreciate living around. Although the public transport can be difficult and traveling to different parts given the distances and traffic gridlock may seem impossible, plunge into as many of the icons of LA as possible. Take as much time as you can touring them, or come back as often as possible to do a bit at a time. Also try the former homes of the famous residents, such as the Getty Estate, which will give you a real flavor of the people who made the city what it is.

The six accessible sites chosen for your Los Angeles (LA) tour are the following:

Los Angeles County Museum of Art (The County)

5905 Wilshire Blvd
Los Angeles, CA 90036
Tel: 323 857 6109

The County is said to be the largest art museum in the western US, and it has more than 142,000 pieces dating back to around 4000 BC. As I write this, the museum is in the process of unifying its whole site, including other institutions such as The Broad, which is featured below. The County was originally opened as the Los Angeles Museum of History, Science, and Art in 1910. It changed its name to the Los Angeles County Museum of Art in 1961 and became a separate, art-focused institution from then on. The County opened its new Wilshire Boulevard complex to the public in 1965 on what is now a twenty-acre site. From then on, it hosted its permanent collection in The Ahmanson Building, held special exhibitions in the Hammer Building, and staged public programs, lectures, and so forth in the 600-seat Bing Theater.

The Broad

221 S Grand Ave
Los Angeles, CA 90012
Tel: 213 232 6200
info@thebroad.org

This is a large modern art museum, with free general admission for its 800,000 annual visitors and 120,000 square feet of public space over two floors. The Broad features two thousand artworks from its own collection, with work dating from the 1950s onward—so this is a very contemporary art museum. The Broad Art Foundation, which funds the museum, also has a lending library that has been active since 1984 and loans its works internationally. The museum was founded by Eli and Edythe Broad in Grand Avenue, LA. Part of the joy of visiting The Broad is its main building, which is an angular, floating, ethereal palace designed by Diller Scofidio + Renfro with Gensler.

The Huntington

1151 Oxford Rd
San Marino, CA 91108
Tel: 626 405 2100

The Huntington is more than an art and botanical museum, it is a monument to a famous family of collectors and its encyclopedic collections. Based in San Marino on the outskirts of LA, each year it has more than 750,000 visitors and is the intellectual home of 1,700 scholars.

Founded by Henry and Arabella Huntington in 1919, The Huntington runs as a not-for-profit organization featuring books, manuscripts, artworks, and a botanical collection on its 120-acre site. It was founded to be a cultural site for the "advancement of learning, the arts and sciences, and to promote the public welfare."[1] With this original purpose in mind, The Huntington evolved into The Huntington Library, Art Collections, and Botanical Gardens.

The Getty Center (The Getty)

1200 Getty Center Dr
Los Angeles, CA 90049
Tel: 310 440 7300

The Getty, formally known as the J. Paul Getty Museum Trust, is an arts and cultural institution founded by billionaire J. Paul Getty in 1953. The Getty has almost two million visitors every year in the buildings and gardens in its Getty Center and Getty Villa combined. The first J. Paul Getty Museum opened in Getty's home in Malibu. Following his death, Getty's estate became the current trust in 1982, and renamed the J. Paul Getty Trust in 1983. Money from this trust sponsored the Getty Villa, Pacific Palisades, and a Getty Center in the suburb of Brentwood. Getty's estate subsequently led to the foundation of the Getty Conservation Institute, the Getty Research Institute, and the Getty Foundation.

Ahmanson Theatre (The Ahmanson)

135 N Grand Ave
Los Angeles, CA 90012
Tel: 213 628 2772

In comparison to many of the other grand theaters featured in this book, The Ahmanson is a relatively modern site with a capacity of just over 2,000 for each performance. The resident theatrical company is the Center Theatre Group, founded by Gordon Davidson. The group has since developed a number of renowned productions, including musicals that moved on to Broadway. The Ahmanson was founded by Howard F. Ahmanson Sr., an insurance and savings and loans magnet in the early 1960s. The theater is named after his wife, Caroline Leonetti Ahmanson. Building work for The Ahmanson began in 1962, and it staged the first of its productions of its now many dramas, musicals, and comedies in 1967. The 1960s building was renovated in the 1990s, increasing its capacity.

Hollywood Pantages (The Pantages)

6233 Hollywood Blvd
Los Angeles, CA 90028
Tel: 323 468 1770

Not just a famous LA theater, The Pantages holds an almost legendary status in the pantheon of US live entertainment and cinematic history and culture. Opened as a movie theater on Hollywood Boulevard in 1930, it cost $1.25 million to build and furnish, a fortune at the time. The Pantages was also the home of the Academy Awards and the Oscars for ten years. Howard Hughes bought the theater in 1949 and changed its name to the RKO Pantages and its performance focus to mostly live shows. Pacific Theatres subsequently bought The Pantages from RKO in 1967, reverted the theater to its original name, and commissioned its refurbishment in 2000. This refurb took the theater back to its original 1930s plaster work, gold leafing, plush seating, and carpeting in the modern era. In honor of its history and in recognition of its refurbishment, in 2001 The Pantages had a Preservation Award granted by the Los Angeles Conservancy.

ACCESS FOR VISITORS WITH SIGHT LOSS

The Broad has large-print gallery notes for people with visual access issues and typed transcripts of its audio tours. All this accessible information is available to borrow free from visitor services associates after entering the gallery but is not bookable in advance.

The Getty has a downloadable app called the GettyGuide®, which gives largely accessible information about its collection and provides audio descriptions of its artworks. The audio descriptions on the app highlight narratives by curators, conservators, and artists on special exhibits and are available in a number of languages. It is also possible to coordinate the Getty-

Guide during your visit, and you can borrow iPod Touches with the app preloaded at the museum. This service is free and open to all, including those without access issues, although to borrow these iPod Touches you'll have to leave official photo ID until they're returned. If you prefer, the museum has more specialized verbal description tours available, which offer detailed descriptions. In addition, The Getty also offers an innovative audio tour for younger visitors with vision loss. For instance, the program Demons, Angels, and Monsters includes verbal imaging of artworks in the museum.

As with audio description described in its information section, **The Ahmanson** offers a weekend matinee performance with ASL on the mainstage for the Center Theatre Group's productions. For information on these performances and tickets, call 213 628 2772. All performances at the museum offer enhanced viewing and instruction through borrowable binoculars and telephones. Specific staff members are not advertised as a point of contact, so visitors should approach staff in the theater lobbies when they first arrive to ask about these services. The Ahmanson advertises a charge to borrow the binoculars, and a California driver's license is needed to prove your identity when you borrow them. The museum also offers audio description during one matinee performance for a number of its own productions. I'd advise contacting the museum at least a month before you plan to visit.

Binoculars and various headsets are also available at **The Pantages** for theater performances. The number of these devices is limited and not free. As with similar sites, official photo ID is also needed for all devices you borrow from the theater. Email PanBoxOffice@HollywoodPantages.com for more details, or call 323 468 1782 during the working week about availability and other access needs. Recently, the theater also started printing large-print playbills, which can be acquired from Audience Services when you visit.

ACCESS FOR VISITORS WITH HEARING LOSS

The County has borrowable assistive listening devices for the Bing Theater. The museum advises asking the security staff in the theater for these devices, and you will need to show official ID before borrowing them. The museum can offer ASL interpretation for tours of the museum through their visitor services. The County also offers tours for visitors with special needs. These latter tours are adapted and can be made available to all age groups. They last around fifty minutes and are led by the museum's own docents. Because of its specialized nature, access tours at the museum need to be arranged with plenty of notice—at least three weeks prior. Call 323 857 6109 or email educate@lacma.org.

As with its contemporaries in LA, **The Getty** offers assisted listening devices for some of its tours and orientation sessions. It also offers induction neck loops for tours and events, text transcripts of its audio tours, and infrared sound systems for events at its Harold M. Williams Auditorium and Museum Lecture Hall. The Getty also offers open captioning for its orientation films. Payphones in the museum also have volume controls for people with hearing loss, and TTY phones can be found in different locations around its site.

ASL tours are also available at **The Broad**. These tours need to be pre-booked, and it is advised that you contact the site at least two weeks before you plan your visit to the museum. For information on these tours, email groups@thebroad.org.

ASL is also available for public events at **The Huntington**, such as classes or talks. Call 626 405 3549 at least two weeks prior to the event. Access at The Huntington can be discussed using the same telephone number, but unfortunately TTY is not advertised. The museum also has assistive listening devices and captions during public events. Again, contact the museum at least two weeks before your visit to arrange for captions and devices.

All performances at **The Ahmanson** offer enhanced listening through borrowable assistive listening devices. Specific staff members are not advertised as a point of contact, so visitors should approach staff in the theater lobbies when they first arrive to ask about these services.

T-coil receivers and infrared listening systems are available at **The Pantages** during shows. The number of these devices is limited. Official photo ID is also needed for all devices you borrow from the theater. Email PanBoxOffice@HollywoodPantages.com or call 323 468 1782. It also has an induction loop for visitors with hearing aids with the T-switch built in, so you simply need to switch your hearing aid to this function if you have it. You can test this loop on request before your show at The Pantages, although again it is advised that you contact the theater beforehand about details of these services. The theater also offers nuanced ASL-interpreted performances, with an ASL seating area for each of these performances. The theater advises that all formal access requests should be made over two weeks in advance, and the theater prefers requests via email.

ACCESS FOR VISITORS WITH LEARNING DISABILITIES, MEMORY LOSS, AND AUTISM HIGHER ON THE SPECTRUM

The County advertises more appropriate times to visit for those who prefer quieter, less crowded, and less sensory-stimulating environments. These times are generally lunch hours to later afternoons, Tuesdays through Thursdays.

The Broad offers social narratives for those with higher-on-the-spectrum autism and learning disabilities. The narrative has expectations and elements of the museum in its story and eases visits to the museum. These narratives look like they are most useful for children, although it's not stated whether they exist (or are suited) for adults too.

The Huntington also has social narratives and is more explicit in mentioning that they are designed for families with children presumably higher on the spectrum of autism, teachers, and supporters. The narrative is available from the museum or can be downloaded from the website.

ACCESS FOR VISITORS WITH MOBILITY ISSUES

The County states its galleries are all wheelchair accessible. The museum also offers accessible parking in its parking lots on Sixth Street and at Spaulding and Wilshire Boulevard. All restrooms at the museum also cater to wheelchair users and have enough space for people with other mobility issues, including those with sensory impairments. The museum recommends that if you have mobility issues, the best place to drop off before your show is between Wilshire Boulevard and Spaulding Avenue. There is an elevator close to this entrance. Once in the museum, borrowable wheelchairs are free from the Ticket Office, although you must show official photo ID to borrow one.

The Broad offers accessible parking spaces in its garage for automobiles showing disability placards or license plates. Similarly, once in the museum all the public spaces in the museum are navigable via wheelchairs, scooters, and so forth. As with The County, there are drop-off points outside the museum's entrance for people with mobility issues. It is advised you contact the museum before your visit for precise details.

The Huntington also has its own free borrowable wheelchairs. I'd advise contacting the museum before you plan to visit for information about this. Additionally, there is a small shuttle bus for folks who need extra help with mobility around its campus. This shuttle is free, runs around every thirty minutes, and makes stops approximately every thirty minutes. Shuttle signs with SAV are posted around the site, although it's advised that you contact the museum or go to its website before your visit to find all the stops en route and read its rules of travel.

The Getty has plenty of seating and rest areas around its site, access facilities in its bathrooms, and, like the other places in this chapter, accessible parking spaces in its parking garage. What's more, the museum also has a family restroom where supporters can help visitors, as well as elevators throughout its complex of buildings and parking garage. In addition, its auditorium and lecture hall have accessible seating for wheelchairs, although it is not wholly clear whether a companion can accompany those in wheelchairs too. Consequently, it's advised that you contact the Getty before visiting to

Chapter Twelve

Miami, Florida

Miami is the most southerly big city on the US mainland, with the most southerly archipelago of Key Largo less than seventy miles to its southern border. It's shaded from its tropical region's Atlantic coastline by its bay and the threadlike Miami Beach, Virginia Key, and Key Biscayne, with their contour of mirror-windowed skyscrapers breaking up its skyline. It's also separated from the swamplands of the Everglades by the vast metropolitan area beyond its city border. This geography has defined its culture and role as a city for vacationers, with its unique wildlife and seemingly never-ending shoreline drawing visitors for over a century. The city itself is modern, only being incorporated in 1896 when it became the terminal station of the railroad in the southern US. From there, the city grew rapidly with its most famous architectural period being the art-deco period of the 1920s to the 1930s.

INSIDER TIP

There are two elements that make Miami a complex and interesting culture.

The first element is its climate and the quality of its light. Perhaps the most pleasurable experience you'll feel when flying in from the northern states in the dry tropical winter is the heat of Miami, which wraps itself around you as soon as you leave its airport. It is a bit like being wrapped in a warm blanket straight from the dryer. The light itself is quite stunning, with the colored buildings looking clean and heat cracks being masked by the sunshine.

The second element of the city is its unique blend of cultures, with a famous Latino-Caribbean quarter, and migration from Cuba increasing rapidly from 1959 after the collapse of its Batista regime. This makes Miami a unique mixture of music, art, food, and street life and, although it is a cliché, it really can be described as an assault on the senses.

For this reason, the sites chosen for your tour of Miami include areas that are close to the shoreline and the bay that is the city's greatest asset. In addition, I've included places that highlight the city's tropical weather and diverse artistic culture, from Native American to Latino to what are thought of as more traditional American artworks.

The six accessible sites chosen for your Miami tour are as follows:

Pérez Art Museum Miami (PAMM)

1103 Biscayne Blvd
Miami, FL 33132
Tel: 305 375 3000

PAMM is based in a modern glass and steel building on Miami's shorefront overlooking the Biscayne Bay, and it has spectacular hanging gardens. Its collections include modern and contemporary art from the twentieth and twenty-first centuries. It was given its current name in 2013 and expanded to its approximately 200,000-square-foot campus including a library, bookshop, and education center on contemporary art. The museum was originally the county's Miami Art Museum and was founded as a partnership between the Metropolitan Dade County government and the Center for the Fine Arts Association, Inc., in 1984. In 1994, it was renamed again the Miami Art Museum of Dade County Association, Inc., and moved to the city's thirty-acre waterfront museum campus.

HistoryMiami Museum (HistoryMiami)

101 West Flagler St
Miami, FL 33130
Tel: 305 375 1492

HistoryMiami is a Smithsonian-affiliated museum based in downtown Miami that narrates the diverse history and modern culture of the local population through exhibitions that it describes as *Miami Stories*. These stories include local historical pieces as well as multimedia and interactive displays. In addition to its site, the museum runs city tours and conducts research on the history of Miami's residents past and present, and its surroundings. The museum's collection was founded by the Historical Association of Southern Florida in 1940, with its first museum being established in 1962 as the Historical Museum of Southern Florida. Following its initial growth, it moved to the Miami-Dade Cultural Center in 1984 and started revolving its exhibitions and expanding its education and outreach programs. In 2010, the organization was renamed HistoryMiami Museum, and in 2011 it became a part of the Smithsonian in recognition of its rich understanding of the local area and its people.

The Bass Museum of Art (The Bass)

2100 Collins Ave
Miami Beach, FL 33139
Tel: 305 673 7530

The Bass is a contemporary art museum and a not-for-profit corporation whose collection includes work by international "mid-career and established artists." In addition to its fine artworks, the museum's collections include architectural drawings, models, and design pieces in its 20,000 square feet of public exhibition spaces. It also runs school programs in partnership with the City of Miami Beach, which it calls STEAM+. The museum opened in 1964 in the Miami Beach Public Library and Art Center with a collection donated by John and Johanna Bass. The Bass building itself was originally built in the 1930s. In 2001, the building was renovated and a new wing was added, representing its growth of both permanent and touring exhibitions. In 2017, The Bass built further galleries and opened its current museum store and education space.

Phillip and Patricia Frost Museum of Science (Museum of Science)

1101 Biscayne Blvd
Miami, FL 33132
Tel: 305 434 9600

Museum of Science is a private, not-for-profit institution in the same waterfront museum park as PAMM, with views of the Biscayne Bay. It features multimedia and interactive exhibitions that cover different topics in the study of science. It also has a planetarium and aquarium. The museum was founded as the Junior Museum of Miami in 1949, influenced by the Junior League of Miami, and opened in a house on Biscayne Boulevard, which was bought in 1950. Around ten years later, the museum was renamed Miami Museum of Science and opened in Vizcaya, where its planetarium was added. In 2015, the old museum building closed to the public and became its offices, learning site, and bird of prey center, with the new public museum reopening on Biscayne Boulevard in 2017.

The Adrienne Arsht Center for the Performing Arts (The Arsht)

Arts of Miami-Dade County, Inc.
1300 Biscayne Blvd
Miami, FL 33132
Tel: 786 468 2000

The Arsht is a not-for-profit arts center, based in downtown Miami and run by Miami-Dade County. Its performance spaces and auditoria include a rehearsal studio, plaza for the arts, concert hall, studio theater, and opera house. The center has around 570,000 square feet of space and stages a little under four hundred events a year, the most prominent of which are music shows. Among its most famous events are its series incorporating jazz and flamenco, reflecting the city's local Cuban and Hispanic populations, and its surrounding square hosts popular events, including food markets. The center also has a performing arts education department, which is said to work with nearly sixty thousand children a year. The center opened in 2006 and is named after its major donor, Adrienne Arsht.

Olympia Theater (The Olympia)

174 E Flagler St
Miami, FL 33131

Mailing Address:

169 E Flagler St #837
Miami, FL 33131
Tel: 305 374 2444

The Olympia is an ornate, highly eccentric theater with a one-off interior design based in downtown Miami that is almost worth the visit without taking in a show. Given its architecture and décor, it is a traditional arts theater, staging plays, solo performers, and bands of all types. As I write, it particularly seems to feature comedy shows in its calendar and has regular free shows on Wednesday nights. The theater is largely supported by grants from institutions such as Miami-Dade County and Culture Builds Florida, among many others. The theater opened in 1926, and despite facing bankruptcy in 2010, it became a corporation and developed the quality of its productions.

ACCESS FOR VISITORS WITH SIGHT LOSS

PAMM's website has accessible information about its collections for people with vision loss. The museum also has regular accessible touch and audio tours, developed by its education department. The tours feature different parts of its collection each month. I'd advise that you contact the museum at least a month before you plan to visit to book a place. Call 786 345 5629 or email elyn-sue@pamm.org.

HistoryMiami has borrowable large-print handouts of gallery text for visitors with vision loss at its visitor services desk. It also has a downloadable, zoomable map in English, Spanish, and Haitian Creole; a downloadable sound map in English, Spanish, and Haitian Creole; and a self-guided audio tour that can be downloaded to your cell phone. The downloadable tour is a little under half an hour long. Many of the museum's exhibits are interactive and generally accessible to visitors with low vision, and it has borrowable tactile blocks for visitors who wish to touch information. Email accessibility@historymiami.org or call 305 375 1492.

The Bass has borrowable large-print text documents at the front desk of the museum and large-print public gallery information in its galleries. Call 305 673 7530.

Museum of Science has a new app with downloadable audio descriptions, text, and video of touch exhibits—as I write this chapter, this app is still being refined. When touring the museum, the items featured on the app have AD symbols that are described on the tour. It also runs regular handling sessions, touch tours, and touch experiences for many of its exhibits including its aquarium, some of which have audio descriptions on their app.

The Arsht has free audio description using borrowable headsets, which are held by the house manager during your visit. I'd strongly advise you to contact the center before visiting for more information. The Arsht also offers touch tour items such as costumes and props—these opportunities are generally advertised on the website, but I'd also advise that you contact the site to find out more. Call 305 949 6722 or TTY: 786 468 2011.

ACCESS FOR VISITORS WITH HEARING LOSS

PAMM offers visitors free borrowable assistive listening devices at its visitor services. If you need accessible text formats, I'd advise you to provide at least a month's notice before you plan to visit to ask for these documents. Call 786 345 5629 or email elyn-sue@pamm.org.

HistoryMiami can arrange ASL interpretation for visitors with hearing loss attending education programs at the museum. You'll need to contact the museum at least two weeks before you visit, although it's advised that you give more notice if possible to request an interpreter. Email accessibility@historymiami.org.

The Bass also has assistive listening devices and ASL interpreters for its education programs and workshops. The museum states that you should contact them to request an interpreter at least two weeks before you plan to visit, and I'd advise contacting them a week in advance for information on devices. Call 305 673 7530 or email info@thebass.org.

Museum of Science offers visitors with hearing loss borrowable assistive listening devices in its planetarium. These devices can be borrowed at the museum's entrance.

The Arsht has free borrowable enhanced listening devices, which can be requested from the house manager when you visit. The theater also has captions during some of its performances on an open screen. Again, I'd advise contacting the center at least a week before you plan to visit for more information. The center also stages ASL interpreters for selected regular performances and other special events, such as show talks. These shows are generally advertised on their calendar and through their website.

Like the Arsht, **The Olympia** has free borrowable assisted-listening devices that can be checked out from the house manager when you arrive. Again, I'd advise that you contact the theater before you plan to visit for more information about these devices.

ACCESS FOR VISITORS WITH LEARNING DISABILITIES, MEMORY LOSS, AND AUTISM HIGHER ON THE SPECTRUM

HistoryMiami has free borrowable noise-reducing headphones and sensory backpacks for visitors with autism higher on the spectrum. These items are available at the visitor services desk; you'll need to leave official photo ID until you return them. I'd advise contacting the museum for information before you plan to visit. Email accessibility@historymiami.org or call 305 375 1492. They also have a downloadable pre-visit guide called "Going to the Museum" and a sound map on the access page of their website for visitors with autism higher on the spectrum and learning disabilities. These documents are all available in English, Spanish, and Creole.

ACCESS FOR VISITORS WITH MOBILITY ISSUES

PAMM has drop-off areas close to its entrance and accessible spaces for automobiles less than eight feet tall with disability symbols in their parking garage. The museum recommends that you contact them before you plan to visit for more information. Call 305 375 3000 or email info@pamm.org. It has elevators in its parking garage to the museum entrance, which has an automatic door, plus elevators throughout its main building. There is also an elevator in its local metro station to street level, leaving a more accessible path to the museum entrance for visitors with mobility issues.

HistoryMiami has accessible spaces in its parking lot for automobiles with disability symbols, and there is an elevator from the parking lot to the museum's plaza—the nearby cultural center also has a parking garage with accessible spaces and elevators to the plaza. Outside, the museum has accessible doors. Inside, it has free borrowable wheelchairs and lightweight stools or chairs at its visitor services desk, although you'll need to give official photo ID until you return these chairs or seats. I'd advise asking about these chairs and seats when you enter the museum or contacting them before you plan to visit for information. Email accessibility@historymiami.org.

The Bass states that it's accessible to visitors with mobility issues. Outside, it has accessible parking spaces nearby for automobiles with disability symbols, ramps, and accessible entrance doors. Inside, its bathrooms are largely accessible. It also has free borrowable wheelchairs, although I'd advise that you contact the museum before you plan to visit for information about this service. Call 305 673 7530.

Museum of Science has a drop-off area near its entrance and accessible spaces in its parking garage for automobiles with disability symbols that are less than eight feet long, and an elevator and ramp to the main museum plaza. Inside the museum, there are elevators on all public levels, a ramp to the aquarium, and accessible bathrooms, some of which have showers. As with other museums, it has free borrowable wheelchairs at its member and guest relations office, and I'd advise you to check when you enter or before you plan to visit about possible further assistance around the building. Email accessibility@frostscience.org. In addition, its planetarium and café have wheelchair-accessible seating and seats with removable arms.

The Arsht has accessible seating and seating with removable arms in its auditoria that can be booked online. Note that there are strict rules against visitors without mobility issues booking these seats, so if you're in doubt if you qualify, I'd advise contacting the theater first. The center also states its public areas are accessible for people with mobility issues.

The Olympia has accessible parking spaces near the theater for automobiles with disability symbols, and there are largely accessible sidewalks and an accessible entrance door. Inside the theater, its bathrooms and concession stands are largely accessible. The auditoria also have wheelchair spacing, and some seats have removable arms. To book these seats and for more information, contact the box office at least a month before you plan to visit, even more for popular shows. Call 305 374 2444.

ACCESS FOR SUPPORTERS

PAMM allows professional supporters to enter free when coming with visitors with disabilities. The extra ticket needs to be requested at the time you book your tickets. I'd advise you contact the site earlier to arrange further support during your visit. Call 305 375 3000 or email info@pamm.org.

As with PAMM, **HistoryMiami** allows professional supporters to enter free if they're supporting a visitor with certain disabilities. I'd advise contacting the museum to find out the specific conditions. Email accessibility@historymiami.org. This free admission needs to be granted through their visitor services and is not applicable to special exhibitions.

The Bass can help visitors with many individual access needs and their supporters during regular visits, although you'll need to contact them before you plan to visit. Call 305 673 7530 or email info@thebass.org.

The Arsht has companion seating near or with accessible seats for supporters, family, or friends. I'd advise contacting the center about these seats or other particular issues on arrival or before attending performances if you or the visitor you support has specific access issues. Call 305 949 6722 or TTY: 786 468 2011.

The Olympia advises you to contact them at least two weeks before you plan to visit if you have specific access needs or you are a supporter. Call 305 374 2444.

Chapter Thirteen

New York City, New York

On the US's Atlantic Coast, New York City (NYC) is a city of five disparate boroughs: Manhattan, Queens, Brooklyn, The Bronx, and Staten Island. There is some debate about when the city itself was founded, but it is generally understood that it was a staging post in the early 1620s and founded as a recognized settlement named New Amsterdam around two years later—this makes it one of the oldest cities in the north of the US. It was given the name—along with its host state—in 1664. Perhaps because of its age and complex history, NYC is unusual as a city. It is also diverse because the city is so spread apart, with Staten Island in particular being well away from the rest of the city, almost a city in and of itself. However, if we are honest about this fascinating culturally, financially, socially, and artistically important city, its center is Manhattan. Importantly, Manhattan is the home of museum mile, with the Met, MoMA, and the Guggenheim—see the discussion shortly. It is also a hub of US theater and literature, and it is home to the nation's financial capital on Wall Street.

INSIDER TIP

NYC's insider tip is a little different from others in this book. My friend and colleague Pamela Lawton, who is a teacher at the Met and works with accessible programs, wanted to recommend one museum, The Renee & Chaim Gross Foundation (526 LaGuardia Pl, New York, NY 10012, Tel: 212 529 4906, email info@rcgrossfoundation.org). This museum is particularly tempting for people with vision loss, as it concentrates on the artist's belief that touch and intimacy with artworks was an important motivation of creativity. As Pamela wrote me,

Just to clarify, though, the three primary reasons I thought of the RCG Foundation are (1) The intimacy of the setting, making it a welcome respite from the rest of NYC cultural institutions, on practical, aesthetic and mobility grounds; (2) Chaim Gross's belief in the primacy of touch in experiencing his work; and (3) Tactile Transmissions. . . .

Chaim Gross said, "I like to carve it [wood] and to judge how the work is going by feeling the carved surface. There is a satisfaction and pleasure in the sense of touch that establishes an intimate affinity with the wood. The use of my hands and the customary hand tools maintains the close contact with the wood that I enjoy." [1]

—Pamela Lawton, personal correspondence, November 2019

Following her email, Pamela was kind enough to put me in touch with Sasha Davis, the director of the foundation and its museum. To Pamela's earlier description, Sasha added,

Pamela noted the intimate quality of the space, which I want to echo. The Foundation provides an opportunity to experience the life of the artist in 20th-century New York in a very personal way, as seen in the private spaces of Gross's home and studio.

—Sasha Davis, The Renee & Chaim Gross Foundation, personal correspondence, November 2019

The seven accessible sites chosen for your NYC tour are as follows:

The Metropolitan Museum of Art (The Met)

1000 Fifth Ave
New York, NY 10028-0198
Tel: 212 535 7710

With its three iconic sites in New York City—The Met Fifth Avenue on museum mile, The Met Breuer, and The Met Cloisters—the museum is one of the largest museums in the world by exhibition space. [2] As I write this, it is the third most visited museum in the world. The Met's major collections are vast and include artworks from ancient Egypt, the US, Europe, the Americas, Africa, Oceania, the ancient Near East, and Asia. There are also arms and armor, costumes, drawings and prints, decorative arts, and works from ancient Greece, Rome, and Islam, as well as contemporary art, musical instruments, and photography. The museum was founded in 1870, although its roots date back to a meeting in Paris, France, in 1866 when a group of Americans agreed to create a "national institution and gallery of art." [3]

American Museum of Natural History (Natural History)

Central Park West at 79th St

New York, NY 10024-5192
Tel: 212 769 5100

The Natural History is located on the western side of Central Park, and it is said to have over thirty-three million objects from natural and human history from almost every continent and outer space. It was also the inspiration for the film *Night at the Museum* and Ross's role as a museum scientist on *Friends* for many years. The museum was founded in 1869 and was signed into law by an Act of Incorporation by the governor of New York in 1871. Its first exhibits were shown to the public in the Central Park Arsenal and then transferred to its current building in 1877. Over the next century, it expanded to include a planetarium in 1935 and its Memorial Hall and Rotunda in 1936.

The Museum of Modern Art (MoMA)

11 West 53rd St
New York, NY 10019

And

22-25 Jackson Ave
Long Island City, NY 11101
Tel: 212 708 9400

MoMA has a significant collection of modern and contemporary artworks in its two sites: MoMA in Manhattan and MoMA PS1 in Queens. Beyond its most famous paintings and sculptures, including those by Degas and Picasso, it also has photographs, designs, media and performative works, drawings, and films. The museum has a library covering more than ninety thousand artists. MoMA opened in an office block on Fifth Avenue, New York, in 1929, with the aim of exhibiting artworks from the modernist era and beyond. In 1932, it moved to 53rd Street in Midtown Manhattan, although at the time to a town house rather than a purpose-built museum. It moved to its current specially designed building in 1939, although this has undergone numerous phases of development and expansion, the last of which opened in 2004. Its Queens museum, MoMA PS1, opened in 2000 after a merger between MoMA and PS1 Contemporary Arts Center.

Solomon R. Guggenheim Museum (The Guggenheim)

1071 Fifth Ave
New York, NY 10128-0173
Tel: 212 360 4355

The Guggenheim in Manhattan is the original of what is now the international collection of Guggenheim modern art museums, based as it is on museum mile, Manhattan. As well as its art collection, the Guggenheim is known for touring collections and special exhibitions. It also runs performances, education programs, tours, artist talks, and movie shows. Perhaps what the Guggenheim in Manhattan is best known for, however, is its spiraling building designed by Frank Lloyd Wright. The museum was founded in 1939 by Solomon Guggenheim to house his art collection, develop new exhibitions, and educate. Frank Lloyd Wright was commissioned to design his new building in 1943, and it has stood almost as it was then—both interior and exterior—ever since, even after its major renovation, which opened in 1992. In 2008, the museum was nominated for a place on the United Nations Educational, Scientific, and Cultural Organization (UNESCO) World Heritage List.

Statue of Liberty (Liberty)

Liberty Island
New York, NY 10004
Tel: 212 363 3200

Liberty is part of a larger national park based on Liberty Island, a small island that's just under thirteen acres in the Upper Bay of New York Harbor—although it's closest to Jersey City, it's designated as New York. The island is close to Ellis Island, which is also part of the same national park, and to get to both you'll have to travel by ferry boat from Battery Park in New York or Liberty State Park in New Jersey. The official title of Liberty's grand statue is Liberty Enlightening the World, which was dedicated on site in 1886 and designated as a National Monument in 1924. Following this, the National Park Service started administering the statue and island in 1933. As I write, the park has not long reopened after significant renovations.

The Lincoln Center (Lincoln Center)

70 Lincoln Center Plaza
New York, NY 10023
Tel: 212 875 5000

Lincoln Center stages performance arts of all kinds, offers advanced performing arts education, holds high-profile business and press events, and screens film shows—it also has open public spaces, which it administers through its campus. The center has eleven resident organizations that stage around three thousand shows a year and run long-running programs and festivals, such as the White Light Festivals, Great Performers, American Songbook, Midsummer Night Swing, Lincoln Center Out of Doors, Mostly Mozart, and Live From Lincoln Center. The center was mooted in 1955 by the Slum Clearance Committee as part of its Lincoln Square urban renewal. Following this initiative, Lincoln Center for the Performing Arts was incorporated in 1956. The New York Philharmonic-Symphony Society and the Juilliard School joined in 1957, and the Metropolitan Opera Association joined in 1959. The center has expanded ever since, with a billion-dollar renovation finishing in 2012.

Richard Rodgers Theatre (Richard Rodgers)

226 West 46th St
New York, NY 10036
Tel: 212 221 1211

Richard Rodgers has staged some of the Broadway district's most iconic shows, such as *Chicago, Guys and Dolls, Anything Goes,* and *The Best Little Whorehouse in Texas*—although it also stages plays and music shows. It is situated in Midtown Manhattan in a historic building with gilt decoration, murals, and deep red seats, in the heart of the Broadway theater district. The theater has never wanted overly large numbers of theater-goers for each performance, and even after renovation it has restricted its seating to just over 1,300. The theater opened in 1925 as Chanin's 46th Street Theatre, although it has been taken over and renamed a number of times in its history. In 1981, it was bought by its current owners, and in 1990 it was given its current name, after the composer Richard Rodgers.

ACCESS FOR VISITORS WITH SIGHT LOSS

The Met has Braille throughout its building and a downloadable audio guide for smartphones, or you can request a device from the audio guide desks and museum stores. The museum also has programs and tours for visitors with vision loss. For example, Picture This! workshops, Seeing Through Drawing, and custom tours include access to the touch collection, custom verbal imaging, and guided touch tours. These programs and tours are advertised on its website, or you can contact them directly; I'd advise you contact them at least a month before you plan to visit. Email access@metmuseum.org or call 212 650 2010.

Natural History has Braille labeling and voice information throughout its building. In addition, the museum runs special tours and education programs for people with sight loss. For example, they have Science Sense Tours and touch exhibits for people with vision loss—for a full list of touchable items, look on the access pages of the website or contact the access department directly.

At **MoMA**, information about artworks is often available in large print or Braille throughout its galleries, and they have free borrowable audio guides. You should also ask staff members in the lobby when you arrive about the museum's large-print and Braille guides. The museum runs programs and tours for visitors with vision loss, such as Art Insight and its specialized touch tours. Information about these events is on their website, although I'd advise you contact the access department for information and book a tour at least a month before you plan to visit. Email accessprograms@moma.org.

The Guggenheim has downloadable audio descriptions of a number of artworks in the museum via its website. It also offers tours, workshops, and audio description. I'd advise contacting the access department about these tours at least a month before you hope to visit, although these are often advertised on their website's access section. The museum also has regular education programs, tours, and sessions for people with vision loss, such as The Mind's Eye.

Liberty has a number of borrowable booklets, such as its Park Brochure, available in Braille when you arrive at the site at its information centers. There are also tactile displays in the information center and other buildings throughout the site for people with sight loss, as well as touch objects in their museum and in the pedestal. There is an audio tour that can be used by visitors with vision loss and their parties who have no access issues. I'd advise contacting the site at least a month before visiting and explaining what you'll need when you get there. Call 212 363 3200.

Lincoln Center has large-print and Braille programs for a number of its shows, and the theaters in the center have access to assisted listening devices. I'd advise getting in touch with the center before your visit to arrange for a headset before you arrive, although there is more information on the website. The GalaPro app also has audio descriptions and dubbing of voices of shows and allows you to adjust the volume as you hear the show. A number of shows also have audio description. Check its calendar or website for details of these shows, and I'd also advise contacting the center directly before you buy your ticket.

Richard Rodgers has audio descriptions dubbing of voices on the Gala-Pro app, which also allows you to adjust the volume when you hear the show. The theater offers some performances with audio description. Again, contact the theater to find out when these performances are before you visit.

ACCESS FOR VISITORS WITH HEARING LOSS

The Met has assistive listening devices that can be borrowed during gallery programs, both special programs for people with hearing loss and regular programs, at the audio guide desks. The museum also has borrowable induction loops and other assisted listening devices from the information and membership desks and some admissions desks, and auditoria for events and regular tours. At the Breuer, the ticketing desk and book bar have induction loops that can be used for tours, programs, and lectures. The museum also has captions for lectures, although you'll need to contact the museum at least three weeks before you visit to arrange this. Email access@metmuseum.org or call 212 650 2010. A number of events at the museum have ASL interpretation and *with and without voice interpretation* as standard, and these are advertised on its calendar or its access webpage. ASL interpretation can be arranged for events, programs, and guided tours. Contact their access department at least two weeks before your visit. In addition, the museum has an extensive range of programs for visitors with hearing loss, such as Met Signs and Met Signs Studio.

Natural History's theater offers captions for a number of films, shown on portable panels that you can get from a theater attendant. You can also borrow captioned glasses in the planetarium for some shows. I'd advise that you contact access before you visit to find out more about borrowing these devices. Email accessibility@amnh.org. Transcripts for some museum shows, events in the planetarium, and films in the theater can be downloaded from the website or arranged through the access department. Assistive listening devices can be borrowed for use in some galleries and auditoria. I'd strongly advise you contact the access department at least a week before you attend to find out where these can be used and for what events, as these appear to vary according to the device. The museum also offers ASL-signed tours, which can be spoken for those who don't sign. These are advertised on the website's access pages, and I'd advise getting in touch with the department at least two weeks in advance for bookings.

MoMA has borrowable assistive audio devices, neck loops that can be used with adapted hearing aids, and transcripts. Contact the access department to find out where these devices can be used and where you can borrow them. Email accessprograms@moma.org. Most spaces where MoMA staff interact with the public in the museum, such as classrooms, ticket booths, and desks, have hearing loops that can work with a range of adapted hearing aids.

The Guggenheim can arrange ASL interpreters for most regular tours if you contact the access department at least two weeks before you visit. It also has regular education programs, tours, and sessions for people with specific access needs. For example, it has ASL interpretation for some regular tours and Guggenheim Signs: American Sign Language Video online.

At **Liberty**, the videos and shows in the information center have captions and subtitles, and videos in the museum have subtitles in many instances. The center also has induction loops, and the videos have audio that is largely accessible through an equipped hearing aid. The site has regular tours that can have ASL translation if you use the contact page of the website at least a fortnight before you visit, and the self-guided tour is available as print for visitors with hearing loss. The contact page for access is found on the accessibility webpage; however, the site does not advertise an email address.

Lincoln Center has borrowable assisted listening devices, and I would advise getting in touch with the center before your visit to arrange for a headset before you arrive. A number of performances have captioning or ASL interpreters as advertised on its calendar and through its website, though you should contact the center directly before you buy your ticket.

Richard Rodgers offers some ASL performances, so contact the theater to find out when these are before booking your ticket. The theater also has free borrowable assisted listening devices for people with hearing loss, and you'll need to leave official photo ID with the theater until these are returned. The theater has a loop system that can be used with many modern hearing aids equipped with the T-switch, and subtitles in different languages for shows can be downloaded on the GalaPro app and read during the performances. If you haven't got a smartphone, or don't want to download Gala-Pro, the theater offers some performances with captioning. I'd again advise you to contact the theater to find out when these performances are before you visit.

ACCESS FOR VISITORS WITH LEARNING DISABILITIES, MEMORY LOSS, AND AUTISM HIGHER ON THE SPECTRUM

The Met has a number of online resources for visitors with learning disabilities or autism higher on the spectrum, such as social narratives, visual checklists, and multisensory and interactive maps. They also run programs for visitors with higher-on-the-spectrum autism and learning disabilities, such as specialized workshops and Discoveries. For visitors with dementia, they run a program called Met Escapes.

Natural History also has social stories and runs special tours and education programs for visitors with memory loss and learning difficulties, such as The Discovery Squad for children with autism higher on the spectrum.

MoMA has a social guide for families of visitors with autism higher on the spectrum or with learning disabilities. It also has regular events for visitors with memory loss and learning difficulties, such as Meet Me at MoMA for visitors with dementia and their families.

The Guggenheim provides a social narrative for visitors with learning disabilities and autism higher on the spectrum that can be downloaded from the website before you arrive. The museum also has quiet spaces for people with access needs who may many crowds upsetting. It has regular education programs, tours, and sessions for visitors with memory loss and learning difficulties, such as Guggenheim for All for visitors with autism higher on the spectrum.

ACCESS FOR VISITORS WITH MOBILITY ISSUES

The Met states that it is largely accessible to visitors with mobility issues, and visitors can bring their own mobility devices if they have access issues. Email access@metmuseum.org or call 212 650 2010. The museum has wheelchair-accessible public telephones and accessible entrances located at sidewalk level, plus borrowable wheelchairs from the coat check. It can be accessed by Access-A-Ride, a public bus service for people with mobility issues. I'd advise you to contact the access department to get more information about this service and the exact address to be dropped off at.

Natural History states its building is largely accessible for visitors with mobility issues, and all its gallery and education spaces can be reached on the flat and by elevator. These elevators have Braille labeling and voice information, and the building has a number of accessible bathrooms. Natural History can also be accessed by Access-A-Ride. I'd advise contacting them for information or to get help for specific access issues. Email accessibility@amnh.org or call 212 769 5250. The museum also has free borrowable wheelchairs at the membership desk and main entrance; you'll have to leave official photo ID until they're returned. In addition, the museum's theaters and planetarium include wheelchair locations, accessible chairs, and companion seats.

MoMA states that all its galleries and bathrooms are accessible to people with mobility issues. It has elevators and accessible entrance doors, and the public sidewalk outside is flat and easy to get around. MoMA PS1 (in Queens) also has a wheelchair ramp outside its entrance. The museum has free borrowable wheelchairs at the checkrooms of both museums; you'll need to leave official photo ID until these are returned. The museum has accessible family bathrooms, although these are not as numerous as the regular bathrooms.

The Guggenheim has a drop-off outside its entrance, although this part of New York has heavy traffic. There are accessible bathrooms close to the bottom of the museum and the top of its spiral, an elevator taking visitors to all publicly accessible floors, and a ramp to its restaurant. There are also a number of benches for visitors with mobility issues throughout the museum. During events such as lectures, talks, and education programs, wheelchair spaces and wheelchair-accessible seating are available, although I'd advise contacting them at least a week before. Call 212 423 3575. The museum also offers a handout for visitors who cannot access its High Gallery because of their mobility issues, with images and descriptions of the artworks in the gallery. It has free borrowable wheelchairs from security staff at the entrance.

The National Park Service asserts that the entrance to Liberty Island and many of the buildings are accessible to visitors with mobility issues. After you depart the ferry, you'll find that **Liberty** has cleared pathways and ramps on different parts of the island, especially around the site of the statue. In addition, the service states its information center, bathrooms, eating area, and many parts of the lower pedestal of the building are mostly accessible and have public seating for visitors who need to rest. The park has free borrowable wheelchairs at its information center, although you'll need to leave official photo ID until the chair is returned.

Lincoln Center's parking garage has accessible parking spaces for automobiles showing a disability symbol, and unlike many other sites it may be possible to reserve parking in advance. Call 212 721 6500 or TTY: 212 957 1709. The center also has accessible entrances and exits with elevators and ramps on or around 65th Street—although it should be noted that not all its entrances and exits are accessible. There are also accessible drop-off points on 65th Street, and it is on the Access-A-Ride route, with stops on Lincoln Center Plaza, Broadway, and Amsterdam Avenue for its library. The center states that its buildings are accessible to people with mobility issues, and its ticket desks are designed to be accessible. The center's theaters have accessible spaces and seats for visitors with mobility issues. I'd advise that you contact the center before booking your tickets at least two weeks before you plan to visit.

Richard Rodgers has accessible seating for people with mobility issues, including accessible areas for visitors with mobility issues and sensory loss, the latter to allow visitors to see or hear the show or interpreter. I would advise that you contact the theater when you book your ticket to ask about these seats and those nearby for companions. Call 212 221 1211 or email help@broadwaydirect.com. The theater also has an accessible bathroom for people with mobility issues, this is near the main lobby, and staff can meet you at the entrance of the theater and help you get to and from your seat. As this is a busy theater, I'd advise you to contact the theater at least a week before you plan to visit to ask about this service.

ACCESS FOR SUPPORTERS

The Met offers supporters of visitors with access issues free tickets if they are accompanying them on entry to the museum. Email visitor.assistance@metmuseum.org or call 212 570 3711. In addition, the museum provides a number of online resources for families and friends who wish to visit on their access webpages. If you want a special tour, verbal imaging, or something similar for a group of visitors with access issues—or a mixture of visitors with access issues and friends and family—then this can be arranged through the access department for a fee. Unfortunately, they can't take groups of more than fifty people at a time. I'd advise contacting them at least a month in advance to arrange such a tour or imaging. The museum can adapt many of its regular education programs or tours if you give enough notice to the access and education department, and these tours can be attended by supporters. The museum also has many regular events for visitors with sensory loss, their supporters, friends, and families.

Natural History runs special tours and education programs for people with specific access needs and their friends, families, and supporters. Contact the museum at least a month before you plan to visit. Email accessibility@amnh.org or call 212 769 5250. In addition, the museum's theaters and planetarium offer companion seats with its accessible seating and spaces.

MoMA also offers supporters of visitors with access issues a free ticket if they are with the visitor they support. They have customized tours and art classes with accessible teaching for small groups of visitors with access needs and their friends, families, and supporters. I'd advise you contact the museum at least a month before you plan to visit to ask for information about this. If you live in or around New York, you can also request a visit from the museum for a school or community group.

The Guggenheim offers supporters of visitors with access needs a free ticket if they are supporting the visitor. The person with the access needs will have to ask for a supporter ticket when he or she buys or is given his or her own ticket.

Lincoln Center can be contacted about specific access needs for visitors or their supporters visiting as a group, large or small. Call 212 875 5375. In addition, Lincoln Center can adapt regular tours with touch objects and assisted listening devices—as always, I'd advise letting the center know more than two weeks before you visit. The center has a number of education programs for visitors with access needs and their friends, families, and supporters. These programs are mainly by age group rather than access need, such as Passport to the Arts and Meet the Artist School Series for children with access needs and their families. I'd advise calling at least a month before you plan to visit for information and to book. Email MeetTheArtist@lincolncenter.org or call 212 875 5377.

Chapter Fourteen

Philadelphia, Pennsylvania

Philadelphia borders the wide River Delaware and faces New Jersey on its opposite western river bank. Like other historically important northeastern cities like New York and Boston, it has an old town by its harbor, with more modern skyscrapers in the downtown area that spread out from its historical core. Beyond this commercial area that faces the river, the city's suburbs and neighborhoods reach out into rural and industrial Pennsylvania. The original settlement that was to become Philadelphia was first established as a trading post in the early 1680s, after Charles II, then king of the British Isles, granted the colony of Pennsylvania to William Penn in 1681. From this foundation, Philadelphia became one of the largest, wealthiest, and most politically important cities in pre-independence America. It was known for building ships and, sadly, selling slaves—a title that it held until the nineteenth century when New York took on this symbolic mantle. In the eighteenth century, Philadelphia was perhaps best known for its part in the War of Independence and its place in founding the modern US.

INSIDER TIP

I like modern-day Philadelphia. It's a historical, blue-collar city that doesn't take itself too seriously, and it is often more beautiful than it makes itself out to be. I remember seeing one of my all-time favorite T-shirt slogans in Philadelphia: "New York: Our Crack Whores Can Take Your Crack Whores." The city's not fancy, it's not as bad as this T-shirt made it out to be, it occasionally runs itself down, and, most importantly, it laughs at itself.

Admittedly, all these things combined don't make for much of a vacation-selling recommendation, but to dismiss Philadelphia is to miss out on the early pumping heart of the US. Its buildings, intellect, and rebellious spirit that rarely stands on ceremony make it a great town to visit.

Culturally, when I think of Philadelphia's museums and theaters, I think of the friends and colleagues that I've met with there, especially those who've given me such great advice on access. Although not the first in the field of making museums and theaters accessible, typically Philadelphia has gone against the trend and led the way in a number of great initiatives.

Perhaps the best place to visit for access initiatives is the Philadelphia Museum of Art (PMA), whose steps Rocky climbed so powerfully in that legendary movie scene—and that I tried to re-create badly on first visiting the museum.

When I was starting out in access studies, Carol Whisker was running pioneering programs and tours for people with access needs at the museum. She was one of the first people that I made a point of meeting to learn about these programs and to talk to about the philosophy of *visiting* that the museum promoted.

Although this was many years ago and Carol has long handed over the reins of access, the PMA's programs are still strong and more importantly have influenced many other museums in the area. For this reason alone—2nd there are so many others—Philadelphia is an interesting and reliable place to visit if you have access needs.

The seven accessible sites chosen for your Philadelphia tour are as follows:

Philadelphia Museum of Art (PMA)

2600 Benjamin Franklin Pkwy
Philadelphia, PA 19130
Tel: 215 763 8100

PMA has more than 240,000 artworks and historical pieces and around 200,000 documents of varying kinds in its library and archives. Its artworks are sometimes called a collection of collections, with around 65 percent of them either being given or bequeathed to the museum. Its artworks are also highly comprehensive, covering as they do almost four thousand years of humanity, while its exhibits include re-created period rooms with pieces recovered from historical houses. As with many similar museums, it curates its collections according to media, period, and region, with its most comprehensive pieces being American Art, East Asian Art, European Decorative Arts, Costume and Textiles, Prints, Drawings, and Photographs. Highlights of these collections include its American paintings, sculptures, furniture, silver, and ceramics, along with the European old masters and impressionist paintings and sculptures. The museum was founded after the Centennial

Exhibition of 1876 in Fairmount Park and moved to its current neoclassical building on Benjamin Franklin Parkway in 1928.

The Franklin Institute (The Franklin)

222 North 20th St
Philadelphia, PA 19103
Tel: 215 448 1200

With over 450,000 square feet of public gallery spaces, The Franklin is a voluminous science museum that plays a significant role in local science education. The museum is named in honor of Benjamin Franklin, one of independent America's first scientists and politicians, who lived in Philadelphia as an adult. As I write this chapter, the museum features twelve significant exhibitions, featuring current and past scientific discoveries. The institute was founded in 1824 by local philanthropists and community elders. Within a few years, it was holding public lectures and exhibitions and founding a high school, a library, and a research journal. What is now its museum opened to the public in 1934 as a *Wonderland of Science*. In the late 1990s and early millennium, the institute raised new funds to enable them to expand their exhibition space and add two auditoria, an IMAX screen, and a planetarium.

The Academy of Natural Sciences of Drexel University (The Academy)

1900 Benjamin Franklin Pkwy
Philadelphia, PA 19103
Tel: 215 299 1000

The Academy has a collection of more than eighteen million specimens and archived pieces, including dinosaur skeletons, fossils, and live butterflies. As well as their place as exhibits, these specimens are used for and are the products of research projects by Drexel University and working scientists based in the museum. A significant part of its earliest collection is from the founding fathers of independent America, including Thomas Jefferson, John James Audubon, Meriwether Lewis, and William Clark. The museum was founded in 1812 as a public institution for the development and promotion of the academic sciences that engages with the public. After almost a century of expansion, in 2011 it developed a formal affiliation with Drexel University.

Please Touch Museum (Please Touch)

Memorial Hall
4231 Avenue of the Republic

Philadelphia, PA 19131
Tel: 215 581 3181

Please Touch is housed in the art gallery of the 1876 Centennial International Exhibition, which was also originally the home of the PMA. The museum is a member of the American Alliance of Museums, with its last reported visitor figures being over half a million visitors per year. It is also known as a promoter of children's literature and has a publishing award for young readers. The museum describes itself as a hands-on discovery center designed to promote child-centered, multisensory learning experiences. Perhaps more than most children's museums, this site is less of a museum, with its emphasis being on movement and what it describes as *Whole-Body Learning*. The museum was founded in 1976 on the principles of Montessori education. It then moved to the city's Cherry Street in 1978 as the Please Touch Museum. In 1983, it got a much larger building in Philadelphia's museum district not far from its current site, and moved again in 2008 to its current building.

National Historical Park, Pennsylvania (Historical Park)

143 S 3rd St
Philadelphia, PA 19106
Tel: 215 965 2305

Historical Park is designated a national park, with more than twenty buildings and monuments sited in Philadelphia's historical city center, all of which date back to the War of Independence. Its visitor center is on the original town's Market Street. One of its more famous monuments is the Liberty Bell, which has its own visitor center—although perhaps the most important monument for Philadelphians in the park is Independence Hall, which acted as the center of Philadelphia's community. In addition, the park includes a number of museums, including a Benjamin Franklin Museum and a New Hall Military Museum, as well as the Independence Archaeology Laboratory. The park was authorized as a historical park by Congress in 1948 and was established as a national historical park in 1956. In 1979, Independence Hall was listed as a UNESCO World Heritage Site.

Walnut Street Theatre (Walnut Street)

825 Walnut St
Philadelphia, PA 19107
Tel: 215 574 3550

Walnut Street is the oldest functioning theater in the US. It still stages nationally touring plays, musicals, and stand-up shows and is known as the State Theatre of Pennsylvania. The site stages more than six hundred shows of more than twenty productions per year and accommodates more than 350,000 visitors per theatrical season. The theater is also home to the Walnut Street Theatre School, which educates around 1,200 students per year and runs outreach for up to 100,000 people annually. The theater opened in 1809 and remains largely unchanged since it was first built. In more recent years, it was officially recognized as a National Historic Landmark, and still maintains many of the original interior design features. It established its theater school in 1984.

Kimmel Center, Inc. (The Kimmel)

Center:

> 300 S Broad St
> Philadelphia, PA 19102

Admin:

> 1500 Walnut St, Floor 17
> Philadelphia, PA 19102
> Tel: 215 790 5800 / 215 893 1999

The Kimmel is a mixed performing arts center that stages plays, classical and contemporary music, opera, and ballet. It is made up of a music academy with around 2,900 seats, a main hall with around 2,500 seats, two smaller theaters, and a small studio, which it describes as a *black box* theater. Its Academy of Music is owned by the Philadelphia Orchestra, and the center's resident companies include The Philadelphia Orchestra, the Philly Pops®, PHILADANCO, The Chamber Orchestra of Philadelphia, The Philadelphia Chamber Music Society, Curtis Institute of Music, Opera Philadelphia, and Pennsylvania Ballet. The center was founded in 1996 when The Philadelphia Orchestra bought its site on Broad and Spruce Streets and partnered with the Mayor's Office to build its complex of performance spaces.

ACCESS FOR VISITORS WITH SIGHT LOSS

PMA has free borrowable large-print, Braille, and raised-line maps of the museum at its information desks. For other, more specialized large-print and Braille materials, the museum needs three weeks' notice before you visit to commission or produce these materials. Call 215 684 7602 or email AccesProg@philamuseum.org. The museum also has free audio-described tours using devices at the visitor services desk, as well as handling tours with materials such as touchable graphics and visual descriptions available before the tour. I'd advise contacting the museum at least a month before you plan to visit for information and to book.

The Franklin provides guides for larger groups that have visitors with vision loss, as long as you can contact them at least two weeks before you plan to visit to book. Call 215 448 1226. Small groups and individuals can also book verbal descriptions for a fee, and again you'll need to contact the museum at least two weeks before you plan to visit to book. Email visitorservices@ansp.org or call 215 299 1000. As with many other science institutes, many of the regular activities are more accessible to people with vision loss. Perhaps the best examples are the children's discovery center, exhibits with pieces that can be handled or smelled, and the dinosaur hall with touchable skulls and other hands-on displays.

As the name suggests, at **Please Touch** almost all the exhibits can be touched as a matter of course and are instantly more accessible to visitors with vision loss.

Historical Park has touchable reproductions of historical items in a number of its buildings. It also has audio description for films in the Benjamin Franklin Museum and Independence Visitor Center, and for exhibits at the Germantown White House. You can ask staff about this service when you visit. The museum also has borrowable Braille park maps in its Liberty Bell Center, Congress Hall, Visitor Center, Benjamin Franklin Museum, and Independence Hall. You'll again need to ask staff for these at these sites.

Walnut Street has a number of audio-described shows, which are advertised in its calendar or on its website. I'd advise you to contact the theater for information and booking. Call 215 574 3550. The theater also has borrowable assistive listening devices; I'd advise contacting the house manager at least a week before you plan to visit for information.

The Kimmel has some audio-described shows, including descriptions of props, sets, costumes, and what the venue looks like. These shows are advertised in its calendar and on its website. I'd advise you to contact the center at least a month before you plan to visit for information and booking. Call 215 790 5800. The center also has borrowable Braille and large-print programs at its patron services. Again, contact the center at least a week before you visit for information.

ACCESS FOR VISITORS WITH HEARING LOSS

PMA can arrange ASL interpretation if you're attending education programs or tours. I'd advise you to contact the museum at least two weeks before you plan to visit for information and to book. Call 215 684 7602 or email AccessProg@philamuseum.org. The museum also has borrowable assistive listening devices and scripts for tours, which you can ask your guide for when you take your tour, or you can substitute the script for an audio guide. Contact the museum at least a week before your visit to ask for these services to be made available. In its galleries, many regular videos have captions.

The museum also offers customized tours with more visual props and examples, which are particularly useful for a group of visitors with hearing loss. These tours need to be booked at least a month before you plan to visit. More specialist ASL-interpreted tours also run regularly, and these are advertised on the museum's access webpage (https://philamuseum.org/visit/accessibility).

The Franklin has free borrowable assistive listening devices for its theaters, planetarium, and IMAX® shows at the information desk. You'll need to leave official photo ID until they're returned. The museum also has a screen with captions for accessible seats in the planetarium shows, which you'll need to arrange with the information booth before you visit—the museum asks you to arrive fifteen minutes before your show. For shows and education programs where there are no captions, the museum can arrange ASL interpreters instead, although you'll need to request this service three weeks before you plan to visit. Call 215 448 1226 or use TTY.

The Academy also arranges free ASL interpreters for tours, lectures, and other education programs if it's contacted beforehand. I'd advise contacting them at least a month before you plan to visit. Email reservations@ansp.org or call 215 299 1060.

Walnut Street has borrowable assisted listening devices in its lobby. I'd strongly advise getting to the theater at least half an hour before your show to arrange this, and contact the theater before you plan to visit for information. Call 215 574 3550. The theater also has shows with captions, which are advertised on its calendar and website. Again, I'd advise contacting the theater at least a month before your show for information.

The Kimmel has ASL-interpreted shows and shows with captions advertised through their calendar and on their website. The center states that you'll need to contact their patron services to explain your access needs and to book tickets at least two weeks before you plan to visit. The center also has borrowable assistive listening devices that can be arranged through the house management, although these vary in its different theaters, auditoria, and spaces. With all these services, I'd advise contacting the center before you plan to visit for more information. Call 215 790 5800.

ACCESS FOR VISITORS WITH LEARNING DISABILITIES, MEMORY LOSS, AND AUTISM HIGHER ON THE SPECTRUM

PMA has programs for visitors with learning disabilities and memory loss. It also has a range of education programs, including tours and art-making sessions. For instance, the museum has Sensory Friendly Mornings for visitors with autism higher on the spectrum and their families, with activities and tours. You'll need to contact the museum before to book, I'd advise at least a month before you plan to visit. Call 215 684 7602 or email AccesProg@philamuseum.org.

The Franklin states that visitors with autism higher on the spectrum will find it quieter on weekends and in the afternoon throughout the week. The museum also has Sensory-Friendly Sundays, with quiet, calm spaces and adapted exhibitions. I'd advise that you contact the museum at least a month before you plan to visit for information and to book. If you wish to tour independently, it has borrowable sensory backpacks for visitors with autism higher on the spectrum and learning disabilities at its information desks. The backpacks have devices to reduce sensory stimulation and maps.

The Academy states that the museum is usually quieter for visitors with autism higher on the spectrum after 1:00 in the afternoon. They also run a program called Access to Science for visitors with autism higher on the spectrum. I'd advise you contact them to book this program at least a month before you plan to visit. Call 215 299 1060 or email AccessToScience@ansp.org. The museum also has downloadable social stories, which it calls museum stories, to help prepare children with autism higher on the spectrum or learning disabilities for their visit. These stories can be downloaded from its accessibility webpage (https://ansp.org/visit/plan/accessibility/).

Please Touch has educational programs for visitors with learning disabilities. For example, Play Without Boundaries is for visitors with autism higher on the spectrum and learning disabilities. During this program, the museum is closed to the public and can include special tours, performances, quieter areas, and social stories—the stories are provided ahead of time. I'd advise contacting the museum at least a month before you visit for information and to book. Email education@pleasetouchmuseum.org. For visitors wanting to come during more regular hours, the museum has quieter areas and quiet kits at its admissions desk.

Walnut Street also has programs for visitors with autism higher on the spectrum. Book these ahead of time by contacting the theater's education department at 215 574 3550.

The Kimmel has a number of shows for visitors with autism higher on the spectrum. These shows are sensory-friendly, have low lighting, are cooler, and have open doors during the shows. These need to be booked ahead of time through patron services. I'd advise contacting the center at least a month before you plan to visit. Call 215 790 5800. The center also has borrowable sensory-friendly kits for visitors with autism higher on the spectrum, for both adults and children, and these can be arranged through house managers.

ACCESS FOR VISITORS WITH MOBILITY ISSUES

PMA has its own parking garage nearby, which has accessible spaces for automobiles with disability symbols. It also has a drop-off area near its north entrance. Inside, the museum states that its public areas are largely accessible to people with mobility issues. It has borrowable wheelchairs near the entrance, elevators, and largely accessible bathrooms and water fountains. The museum can adapt tours for people with mobility issues if you let them know before you arrive. Contact them at least two weeks before you plan to visit. Call 215 684 7602 or email AccessProg@philamuseum.org.

The Franklin has a parking garage with accessible spaces for automobiles under six feet tall with a disability symbol. The museum advises contacting them before you plan to visit for more information. Call 215 448 1391, TTY: 215 448 1226, or email guestservices@fi.edu. Inside the museum, there is an accessible entrance, ramps, accessible bathrooms, and elevators around the building, and its IMAX® theater has an accessible entrance. It also has borrowable wheelchairs near the entrance at the information desk. The museum advises that you contact its guest services before you visit to discuss any mobility issues.

The Academy states that its main building and bathrooms are largely accessible to people with mobility issues. The museum also has borrowable wheelchairs that can be requested from staff at its entrance. I'd advise contacting the museum before you plan to visit for information. Call 215 299 1060 or email AccessToScience@ansp.org.

Please Touch has access spaces in its parking lot close to the building for automobiles with disability symbols. The museum states that it is largely accessible to visitors with mobility issues and has largely accessible bathrooms on each floor, plus accessible water fountains, elevators, and a ramp at its entrance. As with other sites in Philadelphia, the museum has borrowable wheelchairs at its admissions desk; you'll need to leave official photo ID until they're returned.

Historical Park states that most of its building are accessible and that most sidewalks around the park are level, with a number of cut curbs for outdoor exhibits. Where there is no access to upper floors, the park offers images of these floors to visitors with mobility issues. In addition, the park has borrowable wheelchairs at its Independence Visitor Center that can be used throughout the park; you'll need to leave official photo ID with the park until the wheelchair is returned.

Walnut Street has accessible seats in its auditorium, which you'll need to book using an alternative number. Call 215 574 3550. The lower floors of the theater have accessible bathrooms and water fountains. The theater asks that you contact them before you plan to visit if you have particular mobility issues to arrange support.

The Kimmel has accessible parking spaces for automobiles with disability symbols in its parking garage. Contact patron services at the center before you plan to visit for information. Call 215 790 5800. Inside, the center has accessible seats and spaces in its auditoria and performance spaces. These spots can be booked via its regular online ticket site or through patron services. Call 215 893 1999, TTY: 215 875 7633, or email patronservices@ticketphiladelphia.org.

ACCESS FOR SUPPORTERS

The PMA has free tickets for caregivers if they're supporting a paying visitor with learning disabilities or memory loss on educational programs at the museum. I'd advise contacting the museum before you plan to visit for information and restrictions. Call 215 684 7602 or email AccessProg@philamuseum.org.

The Franklin gives free tickets for general entry, special tours, and educational programs to caregivers supporting paying visitors with access needs. You'll need to contact the museum before you plan to visit for information, restrictions, and help with booking. Call 215 448 1200.

The Academy, Please Touch, and **The Kimmel** also offer tickets for caregivers supporting visitors with access needs for general entry. In all these sites, visit their websites for information or contact the site directly: The Academy (call 215 299 1060 or email AccessToScience@ansp.org), Please Touch (call 215 581 3181), and The Kimmel (call 215 790 5800).

Chapter Fifteen

San Francisco, California

Founded in 1776 as a Spanish settlement, San Francisco became the Mission of San Francisco de Asis in the early nineteenth century, from which it now derives its name. After becoming part of the Republic of California, it then became part of the US later in the nineteenth century. The city of San Francisco itself is a relatively small city based on an archipelago that restricts it from becoming larger. But like many other large cities nowadays, it is surrounded by a sprawl of smaller cities that merge into one another. In 2000, this meant that the conurbation of San Francisco, Oakland, and Fremont that surrounds its Bay Area had a population of more than 4,300,000.[1] Although this city was extensively developed in the Victorian era, little remains of this original metropolis of mainly wooden buildings. In this early era, the city was built largely using local wood, which was in abundance. However, in 1906 a large part of the city was destroyed or burned to the ground in an apocalyptic earthquake and the fire that followed it. Consequently, despite its heritage, much of the city's architecture now dates from after this earthquake.

INSIDER TIP

San Francisco is a wonderful city, but it has become considerably fancier since I first visited it around twenty years ago. Where the technology industries and its workers used to only be based in Silicon Valley some ways away from the city, many have now moved into the city and gentrified almost all its districts. This transition has its appeals, but it also means that the city has become more expensive, and what were its more interesting areas have become tidier and more sanitized than they were originally famous for—the original hippy areas are particularly commercialized and have now become more about tourist dollars rather than their early free-spirited ideology.

This is not necessarily a problem though.

Some of the greatest treats that San Francisco has to offer are its views and surrounding beaches, mountains, and green spaces, and the best views of these are from its frequent hillsides. The best thing about these views is that they can also be reached via its largely accessible bus system as well as via automobile. I also find its light railway and subway, the BART, a largely accessible way of seeing the scenery of the bay area, especially if traveling from San Francisco toward Fremont, where it runs above street level.

In addition, San Francisco has great national parks, both in and around the city. These parks are largely accessible to people with access issues, and you'll find that park rangers often go out of their way to support visitors' individual needs during regular visits. This support is a philosophy that the National Park Service has promoted for many years now and has become particularly good at putting into practice. As one ranger wrote me while I was investigating access in California a year ago:

> Our preference is to modify programs open to the general public to ensure they include individuals with disabilities. However, we would accommodate an advance request from groups of individuals with disabilities who were traveling together. For example, if a large group of individuals who are Deaf wanted a tour with a sign language interpreter, a unit would arrange it. In other cases, there are park units that have areas that have been designed to be more accessible than others and tours are offered accordingly.
>
> —"Alfred," National Park Service, personal correspondence,
> September 2018

The six accessible sites chosen for your San Francisco tour are the following:

de Young museum (de Young)

50 Hagiwara Tea Garden Dr
Golden Gate Park
San Francisco, CA 94118
Tel: 415 750 3600

The de Young is one of two Fine Arts Museums of San Francisco. Like the Guggenheim in New York, the de Young is also defined by its building, which is worth a visit in itself. This building is around 293,000 square feet and has gardens totaling almost 85,000 square feet surrounding it. Like many high-profile regional art museums, de Young's collection features textiles and collections from Oceania, the Americas, and Africa. It also has a strong collection of American artworks from the 1600s onward. The de Young was founded in 1895 in Golden Gate Park, which borders the Pacific Ocean to the west, and has been there ever since. In 2005, the de Young museum reopened in its current building on the park's Tea Garden Drive, which is adjacent to the park's Japanese Tea Garden.

Exploratorium at Pier 15 (Pier 15)

Embarcadero at Green St
San Francisco, CA 94111
Tel: 415 528 4444

Pier 15 is a science and technology center and museum that develops creative and interactive exhibits on modern developments in science and technology. It also partners with science agencies like NASA. The museum has tours led by orange-vested high school and field trip explainers at the museum and online. The site also runs education programs for local schools, has hundreds of live exhibits, broadcasts live webcasts, has mobile applications, and uses technologies to connect with worldwide scientific studies. The website is also reported to get around twenty-four million visits a year. Pier 15 was founded by Frank Oppenheimer, a scientist and science educator, and opened in 1969. Oppenheimer developed this site because he was reportedly frustrated by existing science education and created the Exploratorium to allow students to experience science directly.

San Francisco Museum of Modern Art (SFMoMA)

151 Third St
San Francisco, CA 94103
Tel: 415 357 4000

SFMoMA is based in the SOMA neighborhood of San Francisco and has four significant collections based on media and topic. These collections include Architecture + Design, Media Arts, Painting + Sculpture, and Photography from the twentieth century onward. As with the de Young discussed earlier, the building itself plays a major part of visiting SFMoMA, which is only around three years old and fated for its architectural brilliance. Subsequently, its latest attendance figures have risen to more than 240,000 per year. The museum opened in 1935 and has an illustrious cultural as well as aesthetic history, with events such as The United Nations Charter being formulated in its old building in 1945. Its new, ultra-modern, significantly expanded museum building opened in 2016.

California Academy of Sciences (The Academy)

55 Music Concourse Dr
San Francisco, CA 94118
Tel: 415 379 8000

The Academy's main attraction is the Kimball Natural History Museum, featuring scientific exhibitions and educational programs on the natural history of the universe. Like the de Young, the museum is based in Golden Gate Park and has a planetarium and aquarium, a living roof, and over 100,000 square feet of public spaces. The museum was founded 1853 by seven philanthropists as the first museum of natural science west of the Atlantic coast. It originally opened in the city's Market Street, exhibiting pieces including a stuffed wooly mammoth, grizzly bears, and preserved local plants. Much of the original collection was destroyed in the 1906 earthquake, and so a new collection was brought from the Galapagos Islands by its academicians. In 1916, the museum moved to Golden Gate Park and grew steadily over the following decades. After the San Francisco earthquake of 1989, it was decided to construct a new modern building, which opened in 2008.

SHN Orpheum Theatre (The Orpheum)

1192 Market St
San Francisco, CA 94102
Tel: 888 746 1799

The Orpheum stages musicals—including touring Broadway shows—contemporary music, comedy shows, and plays in an auditorium with seating for just over 2,200 visitors. The theater is also known for its shows coming from, and sometimes moving to, Broadway, as well as new plays being premiered. Its Spanish Gothic building is almost worth a visit on its own, as its façade and auditorium are a registered San Francisco Landmark. The theater opened in 1926 and was taken over by RKO in 1929 and renamed the O'Farrell Street Orpheum. It was totally renovated in 1953 to present Cinerama and was changed again in the mid-1960s when it showed movies regularly. In 1976, in recognition of its outstanding building, it was registered with the San Francisco Landmarks Preservation Advisory Board, then granted landmark status shortly afterward. In 1998, it was renovated again, with a substantial $20 million investment from its new owners.

The Curran

445 Geary St
San Francisco, CA 94102
Tel: 415 358 1220

The newly restored Curran has staged almost eight thousand mostly touring performances of musicals, plays, and comedy shows from North America and Europe. It has seating for almost 1,600 guests in its art-deco auditorium, the design of which is almost worth the visit by itself. The theater is named after Homer Curran, who came from a wealthy Missourian family. Curran studied music at nearby Stanford University, moved to San Francisco, and worked in local theater. In 1920, Curran went into business with a New York–based company that was setting up venues throughout the US and wanted to establish a theater in San Francisco. From this early company, the theater opened in 1922 as one of the most popular venues in San Francisco.

ACCESS FOR VISITORS WITH SIGHT LOSS

de Young has borrowable audio-guided tours arranged for temporary, special, and parts of permanent exhibits at its audio guide kiosks. It also has borrowable guides and maps in Braille and large print, and a tactile version of its map, although you'll need to leave official photo ID with the museum when borrowing these pieces until they're returned. There is also Braille in the elevators on site. In the galleries, visitors with vision loss can stand closer to artworks than sighted visitors, although they'll need to arrange this provision with membership and visitor services when they arrive or before they visit. This provision can then be arranged with the gallery security guards. In addition, the museum can organize bespoke verbal imaging and touch tours through its access services. I'd advise contacting the museum at least two weeks before you plan to visit for information and to book. Call 415 750 7645 or email access@famsf.org. It also organizes access days throughout the year when the museum is closed, so ask about those days when you call.

Although it is designed for all visitors, the Tactile Dome at **Pier 15** is particularly accessible for visitors with vision loss. The Exploratorium also has borrowable tactile maps at its information desk.

SFMoMA has borrowable Braille and large-print visitor guides and maps at its information desk. The museum also has an app for Apple and Android devices with audio descriptions of its artworks in a number of languages. More details about this app are on its website. In addition, the museum has borrowable large-print transcripts for special exhibition guides and audio descriptions of artworks in selected galleries on borrowable devices from the information desk.

The Academy has borrowable audio description devices for exhibits, and a number of exhibits which can be touched during regular tours. Staff at the museum can give you information about this access when you visit. The elevators in the museum have voice information, and tour guides throughout the site can provide audio descriptions if you contact them at least two weeks before you plan to visit to request this service. Call 415 379 8000.

The Orpheum is part of the GalaPro app for iOS and Android and has audio descriptions and captions for many performances. Check with the theater about which shows can be accessed on the app. The theater also has its own caption devices for some shows and assisted listening devices, which can be borrowed from staff in the theater by leaving official photo ID until the device is returned.

ACCESS FOR VISITORS WITH HEARING LOSS

de Young has ASL and ASL-Tactile interpretation free during lectures, programs, and tours. You'll need to request this service through the access department at least two weeks before you visit. Call 415 750 7645 or email access@famsf.org. The museum also has assistive listening devices for regular tours and lectures. I'd advise contacting the museum before you plan to visit for information about accessing these devices. Some films in the museum have captions, and the staff can arrange transcriptions of lectures, films, and other events if you request this access at least two weeks before you plan to visit. The museum's FAMSF films in the galleries have captions, and other films have borrowable written scripts or transcripts. The museum's auditorium and theater have captions via iPads and other mobile devices. I'd advise contacting access services at least two weeks before you plan to visit for information on these devices. The museum also organizes access days throughout the year when the museum is closed to the public, during which visitors with hearing loss can take tours with ASL interpretation or follow self-guided tours.

Pier 15 offers ASL interpretation for a number of its tours. You'll need to contact their reservations office at least two weeks before you plan to visit for information and to request an interpreter. Call 415 528 4407.

SFMoMA has free borrowable assisted listening devices for its theater and white box space and ASL interpretation for a number of its guided tours. Devices are arranged through its visitor experience assistants when you visit, and interpreters must be arranged before you go. I'd advise contacting the museum at least a month before you plan to visit. Email visit@sfmoma.org. The museum also has an app for Apple and Android devices, which has transcripts of the museum's audio guide. Borrowable print versions of transcripts are also available for some special exhibitions from the information desk.

The Academy has assistive listening devices for its planetarium theater shows, tours, education programs, and museum visits. I'd advise contacting the museum at least one week before you plan to visit for information and to arrange a device. Call 415 379 8000.

The Orpheum has captions and ASL interpretation for many of its special performances, which are advertised on its calendar and website. I'd advise contacting the theater at least a month before you plan to visit for information and to let the theater know your access needs. Call 888 746

1799. For regular performances, it has assisted listening devices and caption devices, which need to be requested from a member of staff when you visit. I'd advise asking for a device at least an hour before your show, and you'll need to leave official photo ID until the device is returned. The theater is also on the GalaPro app for Apple and Android devices and has captions for its regular performances that you can read on your cell phone.

The Curran also has free borrowable assisted listening devices from the theater's boutique, which can be taken out when you visit for your show. As with many other venues, you'll need to leave official photo ID until the device is returned. The theater also has ASL-interpreted shows and shows with captions, which are advertised through its calendar and on its website. I'd advise calling the theater at least a month before you visit for information and to book. Call 415 358 1220.

ACCESS FOR VISITORS WITH LEARNING DISABILITIES, MEMORY LOSS, AND AUTISM HIGHER ON THE SPECTRUM

de Young has a number of programs for people with dementia and similar forms of memory loss, along with their families, friends, and caregivers or supporters. For example, Artful Discoveries is for visitors with dementia and includes descriptions of artworks in small groups. The Memory Café is a similar tour but for visitors with early onset dementia. The museum also organizes highly specialized tours for different cultural groups, such as the Memory Making Social Outing Tour, which is designed specifically for Cantonese-speaking Chinese Americans with what the museum describes as mid-onset dementia.

SFMoMA has a social narrative for visitors with autism higher on the spectrum and learning disabilities that can be downloaded from its website. Its website also publishes a sensory guide, which tells visitors with autism higher on the spectrum about quiet and less stimulating spaces around the museum.

The Academy has downloadable information about quieter places and visiting times on its website for visitors with autism higher on the spectrum. The museum also has borrowable sensory kits and sensory guides at the coat check when you enter for visitors with autism higher on the spectrum. The kits have instruments to reduce stress and muffle sound at times of sensory overload, and the guides give you advice about which exhibits and areas of the museum provide the greatest risk of overstimulation. I'd advise contacting the museum at least two weeks before you visit for information. Call 415 379 8000.

ACCESS FOR VISITORS WITH MOBILITY ISSUES

de Young has accessible parking spaces for automobiles with disability symbols, an accessible drop-off near its entrance on Tea Garden Drive, and an entrance with semi-automated doors and a ramp. Inside, the museum has accessible bathrooms and elevators to most of its public floors. The museum also has borrowable wheelchairs and stools for people with mobility issues near its entrance, although official photo ID must be left with the museum until these pieces are returned. The museum runs tours for people with mobility issues. For instance, its Well Connected Tour is for visitors who can't attend the museum because of mobility issues, particularly older folk. During the tour, visitors telephone in to listen to museum tours and can look at copies of artworks that are mailed to them. The museum also organizes Veteran's Personal Response Tours at the museum, which allow groups of veterans to choose artworks before they visit that they would like to have described when they visit. To book these tours, I'd advise contacting their access department at least a month before you hope to visit or listen in. Call 415 750 7645 or email access@famsf.org.

Pier 15 has a drop-off area near the entrance of the Embarcadero. The site also states that many of its public areas and bathrooms are accessible to visitors with mobility issues, and they have a disability lift in their foyer. The site has free borrowable wheelchairs at its information desk, although you'll have to leave official photo ID until the chair is returned. In addition, there are benches around the site for visitors who need to rest frequently.

SFMoMA has an accessible drop-off area near its entrance, semi-automatic doors at many entrances, and elevators inside the museum to access the other floors. The museum also has borrowable stools and wheelchairs at its coat checks, although you'll need to leave official photo ID with the museum until these devices are returned.

The Academy has accessible spaces for automobiles with disability symbols and access to the museum from the garage via its elevator. I'd advise you contact the site before you plan to visit for more information, or visit the museum's Getting Here webpage. The museum also states that it's mostly accessible to visitors with mobility issues, and there are a number of ramps and accessible bathrooms throughout its building. The museum's planetarium and theater have accessible seating, and there are free borrowable wheelchairs at the coat check when you leave official photo ID.

The Orpheum has accessible bathrooms and elevators in its building to most public areas. The theater also has accessible seating and spaces, moveable seats, and seats next to these or nearby for companions. I'd advise contacting them at least a month before you visit for more information. Call 888 746 1799 or visit the box office in person.

The Curran has accessible seats that can be booked through the theater's regular online booking service. It also has accessible bathrooms, which are accessible via a disability lift. However, The Curran specifies that items like canes or walkers need to be left with staff when you're in the auditorium. I'd advise contacting them at least a month before you visit for information. Call 415 358 1220.

ACCESS FOR SUPPORTERS

de Young offers discounts for visitors with recognized access needs and access days where supporters, friends, and family can come for free. However, there are restrictions to this policy, and I'd advise contacting the museum before you plan to visit for information. Call 415 750 7645 or email access@famsf.org.

Pier 15 has special rates for visitors and groups with recognized access issues, although you'll need to request these before you visit. Call 415 528 4444. The site also states you can organize specialized support through reservations. I'd advise you contact them at least a week before you plan to visit.

SFMoMA has cheaper tickets for visitors with recognized access needs and their professional supporters. There is also a reduced charge for visitors from not-for-profit and social services agencies. I'd advise contacting the museum at least two weeks before you plan to visit. Email visit@sfmoma.org.

The Academy offers free tickets to supporters of visitors with access needs. I'd advise contacting the museum at least two weeks before you plan to visit for restrictions to this policy and information. Call 415 379 8000.

Chapter Sixteen

Seattle, Washington

Seattle is in King County, borders Puget Sound, and is the most northerly large city on the western side of the US. It is shielded from the winds of the Pacific coastline by Olympic National Park, which it faces across the sound, and the Cascade Mountains to the east. This provides Seattle with a temperate but rainy climate—it has one of the highest levels of rainfall in the US—and a green and lush environment. Seattle is named after a Native American leader and is a relatively modern city being originally settled in 1851 as a western port that became a city in 1869. Although its early local industry was largely shipping, agriculture, and logging, later in the twentieth century it also became known as an engineering and technology hub, and most particularly for Microsoft and Boeing. The city of Seattle is also relatively small, with a population of just over 720,000; however, its sprawling urban area, which includes Tacoma and Bellevue, has a population of just short of 3.5 million.[1]

INSIDER TIP

The things that I remember most about arriving in Seattle for the first time almost thirty years ago are its rain and its beauty. Of course, it was a very different Seattle at the time. It was a city of grunge and looked slightly run down, but it had a dynamic energy that seemed to belie what could have been interpreted as an atmosphere of despair. Arriving on a Greyhound as a young man, I had just traveled over the Cascade mountain range that frames the buildings to the east and looks over the city like an elder cousin.

Nowadays, Seattle is of course still very wet. It has some of the highest rainfall in the US, and when it rains, it just rains and rains for an entire day. However, its indoor culture has now been adapted, evolved, and even celebrated. This adaptation has been helped by its successful modern businesses and philanthropic culture that have led to a cluster of interesting indoor sites with an emphasis on intellectual development. It also has interesting food markets that showcase amazing seafood and dairy that are the outcome of so much water above and around.

There is one extra trip that I'd recommend you do when you visit Seattle. This is to tour its seafront, particularly in the shoreline parkland to the north of the city. It's true it doesn't have beach areas with white sand and outdoor bars; in fact, it could be said it isn't always an ideal vacation destination. However, it is one of the few big cities in the US where you can look out over its bay and see forests and mountains plunging down into the sea, or go into one of its skyscrapers or the space needle and see a volcano in one of the country's true last wildernesses.

The six accessible sites chosen for your Seattle tour are as follows:

Seattle Art Museum (SAM)

1300 First Ave
Seattle, WA 98101
Tel: 206 654 3100
TTY: 206 654 3137

SAM's main museum is located downtown and has a global collection curated through cultural histories. These collections include contemporary, Asian, African, Mediterranean, European, Islamic, Oceanic, American, and decorative artworks. It's aware of its place within Native American history and acknowledges its site is on Native land. It also highlights Native American and Australian Aboriginal artworks. Its last published report shows around 428,000 visitors a year.[2] The museum dates back to the Seattle Fine Art Society, which was founded in 1906 and led to SAM's first incarnation as the Art Institute of Seattle in 1933. To expand significantly, a new SAM building opened in 2007, roughly doubling the museum's public space.

Museum of History & Industry (MOHAI)

860 Terry Ave North
Seattle, WA 98109
Tel: 206 324 1126

MOHAI has major collections of photos, books, manuscripts, maps, and objects documenting Seattle's community stories through exhibitions and interactive resources. Its highlights include *True Northwest: The Seattle Journey* and The Bezos Center for Innovation. Its conservation and study of the Seattle-area's history began in the early twentieth century through the foundation of the Seattle Historical Society, which celebrated the founding of what was then the modern city of Seattle.[3] The fruits of this study became the current museum, which first opened in the Montlake neighborhood in 1952. The museum's collection grew substantially in the 1980s, and this growth was followed by a new larger building in downtown Seattle on the site of the Naval Reserve Armory in the South Lake Union neighborhood in 2012.[4] In addition to its less economic social history, the museum also now celebrates its world-famous local industries, such as Boeing and Microsoft.

Pacific Science Center (Science Center)

200 Second Ave North
Seattle, WA 98109
Tel: 206 443 2001

Science Center is said to have one of the most attractive buildings in Seattle, which is housed on a comprehensive seven-acre site.[5] In addition to its regular exhibitions, its highlights include a planetarium, the Tinker Tank, an academy of health & wellness, a tall IMAX screen, and a butterfly house. Many of its exhibits are also interactive, hands-on, or include elements of virtual reality. The museum was founded in 1962 during Seattle's World's Fair, and it rapidly grew to be a significant science education center in the Pacific Northwest working with local schools. In 2010, the center was awarded landmark status by the city's Landmarks Preservation Board.

Bill & Melinda Gates Foundation Discovery Center (Discovery Center)

440 Fifth Ave North
Seattle, WA 98109
Tel: 206 709 3100

Discovery Center has a social remit and was founded to show the "challenges affecting the lives of millions of people around the world."[6] It includes special and permanent exhibits, including interactive portrait panels and hands-on activities. Its exhibits are always based on four main themes: *Our Work* that features the foundation's mission, *Global Challenges* that features challenges by the world's poorest communities, *Fighting Disease* that features the reduction of disease, and *Get Involved* that features actions that visitors can take to make global changes. The center is relatively young, opening as it did in 2012, and guided by its sponsors, the Bill & Melinda Gates Foundation, whose headquarters are adjacent to the center.[7]

The Seattle Paramount Theatre (The Paramount)

911 Pine St
Seattle, WA 98101
Tel: 206 682 1414

The Paramount has dance, comedy, and Broadway shows, plus contemporary and jazz music in an auditorium with just over 2,800 seats. It is the home of the Seattle Theatre Group®, a local company that develops new shows and produces more established pieces. The building itself, which is listed by the National Park Service and is an official city landmark, is worth a visit, and the theater currently has free public tours once a month. The theater opened in 1928 as a movie palace called Seattle Theatre, and early shows included vaudeville and silent movies. In 1974, the building was entered onto the National Register of Historic Places, and in the 1990s it underwent extensive restoration to re-create its original movie palace design. [8]

The 5th Avenue Theatre (5th Avenue)

1308 5th Ave
Seattle, WA 98101
Tel: 206 6251900

The 5th Avenue Theatre primarily stages famous musical productions, including Broadway touring performances, and runs extensive education programs for the local community. Like the Paramount, the 5th Avenue Theatre was opened for vaudeville shows and silent movies. The theater was built in 1926, and its interior was designed to look like the Forbidden City in China. After around fifty years in business, the theater ran into disrepair and was closed in the late 1970s. The theater was then saved in 1979 when local businesses reprised it as a not-for-profit company called the 5th Avenue Theatre Musical Theater Company to stage musicals. After further economic issues in the early 1980s, it almost closed again in 1985 and was only kept in business by off-season theater rentals. After this period, its management changed profoundly in 1987 and it has been successful ever since.

ACCESS FOR VISITORS WITH SIGHT LOSS

SAM has audio guides, Braille instructions, and maps at its ticket desk for a number of exhibitions and borrowable magnifiers to be used in most public spaces, including its library, at its coat check. You'll have to leave official photo ID with the museum when you borrow the instruments until they are returned. The museum also runs a number of special programs for visitors with vision loss. For example, its Art Beyond Sight program includes free adapted tours of selected artworks, which you'll need to book in advance. I'd advise you contact the museum at least a month before you plan to visit for information and to book. Call 206 654 3100 and request the access department. In addition, bespoke individual tours can be arranged for people with sight loss, so contact the museum at least a month before you visit to arrange a tour and describe your needs.

As many of **MOHAI**'s exhibitions are interactive and hands-on, they are often accessible to visitors with low vision if not those without sight. The museum has audio guides in English and Spanish on SoundCloud (https://soundcloud.com/mohaiseattle), which can be downloaded onto your cell phone, and borrowable gallery guides at its admissions desk. The museum also has borrowable exploration and innovation packs for children from different age groups at its admission desk.

As with MOHAI, **Science Center** has many regular exhibits with interactive and audio elements that are largely accessible to people with vision loss. The center also has borrowable Braille guides and a downloadable audio guide. I'd advise contacting them at least a month before you visit for information. Call 206 443 2844.

Discovery Center also has regular interactive, hands-on exhibits that are largely accessible to people with vision loss. What's more, interpretive staff can be made available to support visitors with vision loss who would like to interact and learn from exhibits more easily.

5th Avenue has an audio-described subscription series on a number of shows that can be listened to in many areas of the theater and has dates and booking details for their shows on their website. I'd also advise contacting the theater at least a month before you plan to visit for more information. Email guestservices@5thavenue.org or call 206 625 1900 / 1 888 584 4849. The theater also has free borrowable Braille and large-print programs at its coat check, although you'll need to leave official photo ID until they are returned.

ACCESS FOR VISITORS WITH HEARING LOSS

SAM has information at its admissions desk about assistive listening devices for its auditorium and lecture hall. There is also information at its ticket desk for scripts of its audio tours. It also offers ASL interpretation for its regular tours, although the museum asks that you contact it at least two weeks before you plan to visit to book an interpreter. Email access@seattleartmuseum.org or call 206 654 3123. The museum also has a TTY at its coat check for those who need to make text calls outside the museum.

MOHAI has free borrowable assistive listening devices, including neck loops, at the public programs department for the atrium, conference rooms, and Lakefront Pavilion. You'll need to leave official photo ID until the device is returned. I would also strongly advise contacting the museum before your visit to ask about these devices. Call 206 443 2844.

Science Center has film scripts of IMAX shows in the center before you take your seat, and some of the movies in its theater have captions. You can ask staff about these captions before your show, and I'd advise you arrive at least half an hour before the show. There are also TTY text phones at its information desks.

Discovery Center has assisted listening devices and captions for a number of its own videos. You can also ask for ASL interpreters for public tours and education programs. I'd advise you to contact the center at least a month before you plan to visit to ask for interpretation. Call 206 709 3100.

The Paramount has borrowable assistive listening devices, including loops systems that can be used with adapted hearing aids, at its friends' booth. A number of shows also have ASL interpreters and captions. These are advertised on its website (https://www.stgpresents.org/), or you can visit the box office for more information.

5th Avenue has a number of ASL-interpreted and captioned shows, with accessible seats close to the screen or interpreter. These shows are advertised on its website (https://www.5thavenue.org/promo/?ASL), and you can book these tickets using the code ASL. I'd advise you to contact the theater at least a month before you plan to visit for information. Email guestservices@5thavenue.org or call 206 625 1900. The theater also has borrowable scripts and book lights at its coat check. Visit the theater at least half an hour before your show to request this service.

ACCESS FOR VISITORS WITH LEARNING DISABILITIES, MEMORY LOSS, AND AUTISM HIGHER ON THE SPECTRUM

There are many interactive elements to the exhibits at **MOHAI** that are largely accessible to people with learning difficulties. What's more, the museum has regular borrowable packs for children of different age groups, which also have interactive and tactile elements suitable for people with learning difficulties. These packs are at the admissions desk, and you'll need to leave official photo ID with the museum until they're returned.

Science Center has a number of resources, such as social stories, for visitors with autism higher on the spectrum. These resources can be downloaded from the center's website (https://www.pacificsciencecenter.org/plan-your-visit/accessibility/). The center also has a program designed for people with autism higher on the spectrum called Exploration for All, which gives families the opportunity to visit early at certain less busy and quieter times.

The Paramount has shows that are accessible to visitors with autism higher on the spectrum. I'd advise you to contact the theater at least a month before you plan to visit for information. Call 206 682 1414. The theater also has educational programs for visitors with learning disabilities. For instance, Dance with Life is an outreach program that encourages people in homes or institutions to dance. I'd advise you to contact the theater at least a month before you plan to take a class for information—although if you would like outreach, it would be advisable to contact a number of months before.

ACCESS FOR VISITORS WITH MOBILITY ISSUES

SAM has drop-off areas outside its entrance, and it is close to the local Russell Investments Center Garage, which has access spaces for automobiles less than six feet tall with disability symbols. Inside, the theater and auditorium have borrowable wheelchairs and accessible seating for visitors with mobility issues. I'd advise that you contact the museum at least a week before you visit them for information. Email access@seattlcartmuseum.org or call 206 654 3123.

MOHAI has accessible parking spaces in its parking lot for automobiles with disability symbols, although long vehicles may not be able to enter the lot, as there are size restrictions. There is also a drop-off zone close to its entrance. I'd advise you to check with the museum before you plan to visit for information and restrictions. Call 206 324 1126 and request access services. The museum states it is largely accessible to people with mobility issues, and it has an elevator to all public floors. It also has free borrowable wheelchairs and walkers at its admissions desk, although you'll need to leave official photo ID with the museum until these are returned.

Science Center has an adjacent parking garage with accessible spaces for automobiles with disability symbols, plus a drop-off zone close to its entrance. It also has accessible bathrooms. The center states that many of its exhibits—including its laser dome, planetarium, science stage, and theater—are largely accessible for those with mobility issues. There is also accessible seating in its laser dome, a disability lift on the stairs of its lower levels, benches throughout the center, and elevator access to its IMAX theater. I'd advise you to contact the center for information before you plan to visit. Call 206 443 2844. The center also has an accessibility map on its website (https://www.pacificsciencecenter.org/plan-your-visit/accessibility/) with details about more and less accessible areas, and it has free borrowable wheelchairs at its information desk. For wheelchairs, you'll need to leave official photo ID with the center until the chairs are returned.

Discovery Center has ramps at different points throughout its building and semiautomatic doors outside its bathrooms and main entrance. The center also has a larger accessible bathroom that can be opened by staff members from the entrance or galleries, and it has stools in its galleries for visitors who need to rest. The center also has borrowable wheelchairs. I'd advise you to ask staff about these chairs when you enter the center or contact them before you arrive for information. Call 206 709 3100. If you need particular types of access to one of the center's public programs, you can contact them to make arrangements, I'd advise at least a week before you plan to visit.

The Paramount states that its theater's lowest levels and orchestra floor are largely accessible to visitors with mobility issues, and there are wheelchair spaces and seats. Accessible seats for all shows can be booked using regular websites and ticket lines, although I'd contact the theater at least a month before you visit for information. Call 206 682 1414. The theater also has programs for visitors who are older and find it more difficult to get around. For instance, its Boomers and Beyond is for visitors whom it describes as baby boomers, and the theater offers outreach for institutions such as hospitals for some of its shows. I'd advise contacting the theater at least a month before you'd like a class for information.

5th Avenue is close to local parking garages with accessible spaces for automobiles with disability symbols. The museum also has accessible seats in its auditorium's lower floor, what it calls the orchestra level, which can be booked on its website or through guest services. Call 206 625 1900 or email guestservices@5thavenue.org. There is also a requestable elevator in the theater, although this does not avoid all its stairs.

ACCESS FOR SUPPORTERS

SAM asks visitors with specific access needs to contact them before they visit. Call 206 654 3210.

MOHAI advertises cheaper tickets for groups of adult visitors, allowing people with access needs to visit with families and friends. During these visits, more accessible tours can be requested through the museum. I'd advise you to contact the museum at least a month before you plan to visit for information. Call 206 443 2844.

Science Center has information for those supporting a visitor with access needs or coming with family or friends with access needs. Call 206 443 2001 / TTY: 206 443 2887. Supporters of visitors with access needs also get to visit the center, IMAX theater, and laser show with a supporter ticket. You'll need to contact guest services for information and to book. Call 206 443 2844.

Discovery Center has information for those supporting visitors with access needs before they plan to visit. Email discoverycenter@gatesfoundation.org.

5th Avenue also has information for people supporting visitors with access needs at the theater, so call the theater before you plan to visit. The theater also offers subscriptions for visitors who need regular captions, accessible seats, ASL interpretation, or audio description and information on accessible shows and tickets. Email guestservices@5thavenue.org or call 206 625 1900 or 1 888 584 4849. This service can also be requested through a form on its website (https://www.5thavenue.org/planyourvisit#accessibility).

Chapter Seventeen

Washington, DC

Washington, DC, is the only city to be founded as part of the Constitution of the United States in 1790. Its site was chosen by President Washington, for whom it is named. This means that it was literally designed to become a capital city, unlike other cities that are founded and then become the capital city of a country. Washington is also unique in not being a part of a US state, being its own district, the District of Columbia. The city is bounded by the Potomac River on its southwestern border and sits between the states of Virginia and Maryland—with the Potomac River itself straddling the border between the two states. It is also the first US city to be designed on a grid system, with streets and avenues at right angles or occasional diagonals, and its non-river border is almost perfectly rectangular.

INSIDER TIP

Washington museums are generally accessible. . . . Many of the theaters in DC (Kennedy Center and Imagination Stage in Bethesda) feature sensory friendly shows of their plays.

Tomorrow there is a sensory friendly performance, for instance, of the Kennedy Center's Spooktacular. And the grounds of the center are very wheel-chair friendly, with outdoor sculptures and gardens.

The Sculpture Garden at the National Gallery of Art is accessible and the modern wing has a huge elevator for strollers and wheelchairs—downstairs, below ground, is a huge flat space containing the cafeteria, a roll/walk through installation and the museum shops.

—Natasha Tverdynin, Georgetown University, Washington, DC

The seven accessible sites chosen for your Washington, DC, tour are as follows:

National Air and Space Museum (NASM)

Independence Ave at 6th St, SW
Washington, DC 20560
Tel: 202 633 2214

NASM has air and space travel exhibitions and is said to have the largest public exhibition space of all the Smithsonian museums. The main museum has a site on the National Mall, with a five-story screened IMAX theater and planetarium. It also has twenty-three galleries with traditional engine- and jet-powered vehicles from airplanes to missiles to rockets, plus archives and artworks based on the theme of air travel. Some of these exhibits include famous craft, such as the Hubble Telescope and the Wright Brother's Flyer. Its last advertised visitor figures were over six million a year.[1] NASM opened in 1920 as a large metal building outside Washington. It moved to its current site in 1976 and has continued to expand over the years, with its site in Virginia.

Smithsonian National Museum of Natural History (SNMNH)

10th St & Constitution Ave NW
Washington, DC 20560
Tel: 202 633 5238

The SNMNH helps visitors understand the natural world and our place in it, and it develops narratives on the creation of the Earth itself to current biodiversity. The museum also conducts research in modern-day life sciences, has an institute for children and families called Q?rius, and has halls and galleries featuring human evolution, geological, oceanographic, and fossil exhibitions, among many others. It has a large collection of live butterflies and other insects. The SNMNH collection dates back to the beginning of the Smithsonian Institute in 1846, and its permanent home was opened in 1910 in the center of the city. Since this era, the museum has grown to include an academic library, with holdings from every continent.

The National Gallery of Art and Sculpture Garden (The National Gallery)

National Mall between 3rd and 9th St
Constitution Ave NW
Washington, DC 20565
Tel: 202 737 4215

The National Gallery has more than 150,000 artworks based in two large buildings and a sculpture garden. The gallery hosts educational programs, performances, and movies. It is home to the Center for Advanced Study in the Visual Arts and has an expansive library with an international collection. The National Gallery was founded after the successful lobbying of Franklin D. Roosevelt by the philanthropist Andrew W. Mellon in 1936. Following this successful campaign, the gallery was founded in 1937, and Mellon subsequently financed its first building and donated his art collection, which formed the gallery's earliest exhibitions. Following steady growth, its sculpture garden opened in 1999.

United States Holocaust Memorial Museum (USHMM)

100 Raoul Wallenberg Pl, SW
Washington, DC 20024-2126
Tel: 202 488 0400
TTY: 202 488 0406

USHMM states that it is a living memorial to the Holocaust of Jewish people that occurred in the Nazi-controlled states of Europe during the 1930s and 1940s. Emphasizing the importance of this issue, the museum is based in the National Mall and funded by the government and private donations. The museum also runs educational programs through its Institute of Holocaust Education and conducts outreach in schools and colleges. The museum opened in 1993. It has expanded its programs and exhibitions significantly during its first twenty-five years and has been visited by leading dignitaries as well as the general public. The museum also has online resources about the Holocaust in sixteen languages, allowing access to those who can't get to Washington, DC, in person.

National Museum of African American History & Culture (NMAAH&C)

1400 Constitution Ave NW
Washington, DC 20560
Tel: 844 750 3012

NMAAH&C is a national museum that exhibits life stories, objects, and artworks about the history and culture of African Americans in its voluminous exhibition space. The museum's collection features more than 35,000 objects and artworks and, as it is a relatively young museum, is currently in the first phase of expansion—it's only three years old as I write! The museum also runs regular education programs and has outreach in schools and colleges. The museum is the newest part of the Smithsonian Institute, was founded in 2003 by an Act of Congress, and opened to the general public in

2016. Like other Smithsonian organizations, it was originally founded by a combination of government money and private donations.

The National Theatre

1321 Pennsylvania Ave NW
Washington, DC 20004
Tel: 202 628 6161

The National Theatre stages a wide range of shows, including Broadway musicals, plays, and classical and contemporary concerts in an auditorium with a seating capacity of almost 1,700. The theater runs education programs for children and adults, and it has previously hosted awards, presidential balls, and command performances. The theater was founded in 1835 and is one of the oldest performance venues with touring shows in the country. However, its modern edifice is different from the original theater's, as it burned down on more than one occasion in its 185-year history.

The John F. Kennedy Center for the Performing Arts (Kennedy Center)

2700 F St NW
Washington, DC 20566
Tel: 202 467 4600

The Kennedy Center has a collection of performing arts venues, comprising three main auditoria and nine smaller spaces. It offers mostly musical concerts and shows, including classical, ballet, and contemporary, although it also stages talks, plays, education programs, and a range of shows aimed at different age groups. The center is home to companies such as the National Symphony Orchestra and, as this chapter is being written, it is finishing an expansion that will add open rehearsal and teaching areas. The original center was to be called the National Cultural Center, and its foundation was signed into law in 1958 by President Eisenhower. However, shortly after the shooting of John F. Kennedy, President Johnson helped to rename the center the John F. Kennedy Center for the Performing Arts. The center itself opened for performance in 1971.

ACCESS FOR VISITORS WITH SIGHT LOSS

NASM is on the Aira free app that connects to visual descriptions from volunteers as you tour the museum. You can also get Braille and tactile guides from its Welcome Center, which has information about touch exhibits, audio labels, and descriptions of a number of exhibits. The museum also has audio description for some tours and IMAX theater shows. These tours can be booked through its reservation office. Call 202 633 2563 or email NASMTours@si.edu.

The National Gallery has audio descriptions, podcasts, and gallery talks by well-known figures, as well as audio-described films and an ATM with Braille and audio description. Gallery tours can be made available as Braille transcripts or, for more personalized tours, the site can organize live verbal descriptions of parts of its collection on selected days. I would recommend you contact the gallery at least a month before you plan to visit to get information about these tours.

USHMM has combined audio description and touch tours of parts of its collection. The museum asks that you contact them at least two weeks before you visit to book a place on the tours, although I would advise contacting them at least a month before you intend to visit. Email GHT@ushmm.org or call 202 488 6100 or consult the website, which has a form you can fill in. The information desk offers flashlights and magnifiers for visitors with sight loss, and it has large-print and Braille personal ID cards—personal ID cards are a feature of the museum that tell the life history of an individual from the Holocaust. Visitors can also download audio descriptions of USHMM's halls to their cell phone to listen to them in the museum as they go around.

NMAAH&C has Braille and large-print information and tactile and large-print maps located at the welcome desk. As with other Smithsonian sites, the museum is on the Aira app, and an audio-description tour can be downloaded to visitors' cell phones or tablets. The museum also has staff that can provide verbal imaging of exhibits on request. Get in touch with the museum in advance for information about these tours and to arrange an imaging. Email nmaahcvisitorservices@si.edu.

The National Theatre has some shows with audio description, and I'd advise you contact the theater to find out about these shows and book tickets at least a month before you plan to visit. Call 202 628 6161. The theater also has free borrowable devices and headphones at its coat check. You'll have to leave an official photo ID when you take a device out, and there are limited numbers so they can't be guaranteed.

Kennedy Center has borrowable Braille and large-print playbills for most performances from the usher—but shows featuring only dance are not available in Braille. You can also ask for other pieces to be printed in Braille or large print. Call 202 416 8727 or email access@kennedy-center.org. I would advise that you contact the center at least a month before your visit, particularly if you need Braille, as this can take time to arrange. The center also has audio-described shows with borrowable headsets, which the center asks you check out up to an hour before the show you're visiting, depending on the auditorium. I'd also advise contacting the Kennedy Center around a week before you visit to get information about where and when to pick these up depending on your space or auditoria. Call 202 416 8528 or email access@kennedy-center.org. Outside regular audio-described show times, Kennedy Center also has personalized audio description and touch tours that you can request in your own time. The center asks you to arrange these descriptions at least two weeks in advance through its access office. Call 202 416 8727 or email access@kennedy-center.org.

ACCESS FOR VISITORS WITH HEARING LOSS

NASM can arrange ASL or other forms of signing when two weeks' advanced notice is requested to reserve an individual program or accessibility services. When requesting an accessibility service, please specify the mode of communication required (i.e., state whether you need sign language as ASL, PSE, or Signed English). The museum can also arrange an ASL or other signer for lectures and regular tours. You'll need to contact the museum at least two weeks before you visit. Call 202 633 2563 or email NASM-Tours@si.edu. In addition, the museum's IMAX theater and planetarium have captions for a number of its shows in various languages, and it can reserve seats for visitors with hearing loss to access these captions. I'd advise contacting the museum before you visit for information and to ask about seating. Many of the videos in the exhibitions also have captions.

SNMNH has captions for a number of its videos and hearing loops that work with visitors' hearing aids fitted with this function, which can be checked out from its visitor information desk and theater in the Hall of Human Origins. The museum also has assisted listening devices for its auditorium and Q?rius theater. You can request these devices during your visit. ASL and captioning can also be made available for its regular programming if you contact the museum at least two weeks before you visit. Call 202 633 5238 or email NMNHAccessibility@si.edu.

The National Gallery has ASL videos on parts of its collection, and a number of films on their website and exhibitions have captions. Borrowable transcripts can also be taken out for tours from the Acoustiguide desk. The gallery has borrowable assisted listening devices, neck loops, and headphones for presentations in its Lecture Hall and auditoria. These can be checked out from the information or Acoustiguide desks during your visit. In addition, you can borrow assisted listening devices for regular programs at the gallery if you contact them at least three weeks before your visit. Call 202 842 6905. The gallery also runs tours for visitors who sign in ASL called Art for ASL Learners. This tour is advertised on its calendar and through its website. You'll need to contact the gallery to book onto the tours at least a month before you visit. Places are limited and can't be guaranteed.

USHMM has captions for its multimedia exhibits, and many of these exhibits are equipped for T-switches on hearing aids equipped with this function. Some programs in the auditoria can be accessed through captions, borrowable caption devices, the Web, or borrowable assisted listening devices. These devices are all limited in number and so can't be guaranteed.

Information videos in the **NMAAH&C** galleries have captions, and you can also ask for an ASL interpreter if you are signed up for a program at the museum. The museum asks that you contact them at least two weeks before you visit to arrange for the interpreter. Email nmaahcvisitorservices@si.edu.

A number of shows at **The National Theatre** have captions; contact the theater at least a month before you plan to visit to find out when these shows are and if tickets are available. Call 202 628 6161 or email boxoffice@thenationaldc.com. The theater has assistive listening devices, although the museum advises that you use your own headphones with these devices. The museum also has free, borrowable assistive listening devices and neck loops that are compatible with adapted hearing aids in its coat check. You'll need to leave official photo ID, and their numbers are limited, so being able to borrow one can't be guaranteed.

The Kennedy Center advertises ASL and captioned shows on its calendar, with information about these shows also available at their Instant-Charge Services Desk or by contacting the center directly. Call 202 416 8529 or email access@kennedy-center.org—you can also subscribe to a monthly newsletter of accessible events by emailing the department and adding "Subscribe Interpreted Alerts" to your subject line. You should also note that if you want to request captions or ASL interpretation, you'll need to book seats in the front of the auditoria or performance space. I'd advise contacting the center to find out more information about these services. In addition, you can ask for ASL interpreters, captioning on devices such as iPads, assistive listening devices, headsets, and neck loops for regular performances. Contact the access department at least two weeks before you plan to visit. Call 202 416 8727 or email access@kennedy-center.org.

ACCESS FOR VISITORS WITH LEARNING DISABILITIES, MEMORY LOSS, AND AUTISM HIGHER ON THE SPECTRUM

NASM has information about visits, social stories, and programs for visitors with autism higher on the spectrum and learning difficulties. For example, during Morning at the Museum, families get to attend the museum at quieter times and undertake specially designed activities. The program also has pre-visit information to help visitors' arrivals at the museum. You'll need to contact the museum at least a month in advance to book onto the program. Email access@si.edu.

SNMNH recommends that visitors with autism higher on the spectrum visit between Monday and Wednesday as this is a quieter period, although it is advised to check beforehand as even these days may be busy at different times of the year. The access area of the museum's website also has a recommended tour that allows visitors and their families to choose quieter, less stimulating areas before their visits and to prepare a quieter, less challenging route. The museum also runs programs with interactive touch elements that are more accessible to visitors with learning difficulties. These programs are featured on the Aira Access app, which provides information about the museum for people with learning difficulties and autism higher on the spectrum. Contact the access department for more details. Call 202 633 5238 or email NMNHAccessibility@si.edu.

The National Gallery runs a program called Just Us at the National Gallery of Art for visitors with early dementia and supporters. At the time of writing, sessions for this program run on Mondays twice a month, although I would advise you to contact the gallery at least a month before you intend to visit to book onto the program and for more information. Call 202 842 6905.

NMAAH&C has sensory maps and social stories, which include information on more touchable, interactive exhibits and where there is a danger of higher sensory stimulation. For information about accessing these maps and stories, contact the museum before you visit via email at nmaahcvisitorservices@si.edu. The museum also runs a program called Morning at the Museum. This program allows families of visitors with autism higher on the spectrum to get into the museum with special activities when it's usually closed to the public. I'd advise you check with the museum at least a month before you visit for information and to book onto the program. Email access@si.edu or nmaahcvisitorservices@si.edu.

Kennedy Center has specially organized shows with reduced sensory stimulation for people with autism higher on the spectrum and their families. These shows are advertised on the center's calendar and website. For more general and booking information, contact the center directly by calling 202 416 8727 or emailing access@kennedy-center.org. The Kennedy Center also has social stories for visitors with learning difficulties or autism higher on the spectrum and their families to read before they visit. These can be requested from a special website: www.gettoknowthekc.org.

ACCESS FOR VISITORS WITH MOBILITY ISSUES

NASM has accessible parking spaces opposite the museum for people with disability badges. The museum also has ramps to some of its public entrances, elevators within the museum, and accessible bathrooms and exhibits. The museum's IMAX has seating for wheelchair users. For more information, contact their offices before your visit. Call 202 633 2214 or go to their visitor center when you arrive.

At the time of writing, **SNMNH** advertises that both entrances are accessible for visitors with mobility issues, with an elevated walkway to one entrance. Accessible parking spaces close to the museum can also be found on the National Mall for those with disability badges. The museum states that its exhibitions, theaters, bathrooms, eating areas, and butterfly pavilion have access for people with mobility issues and all its public areas can be reached via elevator. The museum also has free, borrowable wheelchairs near the ground floor entrance. Go to the visitors' desk when you arrive for information about how to take out these wheelchairs.

Two of the main entrances to **The National Gallery** have ramps, and the site also has elevators to public areas, accessible bathrooms for visitors with mobility issues, and a map of the site showing all its accessible areas and facilities. There are nearby accessible parking spaces for those with disability badges on two adjacent streets close to the gallery, plus borrowable wheelchairs near all its entrances. Security guards at the entrances to the gallery have more information about how to access these wheelchairs on your arrival, or you can contact the gallery before visiting for more information. Call 202 842 6905.

There are accessible parking spaces near **USHMM** on the street near the Washington Monument and Independence Avenue for visitors with disability badges. Visitors with mobility issues can also use the drop-off point near its main entrance. The museum states that its public spaces are accessible to visitors with mobility issues, including its bathrooms, and there are elevators to all public floors and ramps where the floor changes height. There are also borrowable wheelchairs that can be taken out from the coat check. I advise you to contact the museum before you arrive for more information about these.

A number of **NMAAH&C**'s galleries have ramps, and its public floors have escalators and elevators. In addition to its family bathrooms, the museum's regular bathrooms have an accessible stall each for users with mobility issues, and their theater has accessible seating. The museum also has borrowable wheelchairs near the Security Desk at the entrance. I'd advise contacting the museum or checking the Smithsonian's accessibility website for more information before you visit. As with the other nearby museums featured in this chapter, there are accessible parking spaces on nearby streets for visitors with disability badges.

The National Theatre has accessible spaces and seats for visitors with wheelchairs in the theater, elevators to all floors, and accessible bathrooms on upper floors. For more information about booking these seats, call 202 628 6161 or email boxoffice@thenationaldc.com.

The Kennedy Center asserts that its public entrances, bathrooms, theaters, and outlets are accessible to visitors with mobility issues. The center also has a parking garage with accessible parking spaces for automobiles with disability badges, elevators from the garage to the center, and a shuttle bus with a wheelchair lift from local metro stations. I'd advise contacting the museum for information about these services around a week before you visit for more details. Call 202 416 8727 or email access@kennedy-center.org. When in the center itself, you'll find elevators between a number of its public floors and accessible spaces and seats for visitors with mobility issues in their auditoria and performance spaces. Contact the center's InstantCharge Services Desk for information about these spaces and seats. Call 202 416 8529.

The center also has borrowable wheelchairs from the visitors' center and, unlike many other sites, you can call to reserve a wheelchair in advance. Call 202 416 8340. The center also has door staff to support visitors with mobility issues from the main entrance of the center to the entrance of their performance space. In addition, from the entrance of each performance space, the center has ushers to support visitors to their seats or spaces—they recommend that if you need support, you should arrive around an hour before your show begins. For more information, contact the center directly. Call 202 416 8727 or email access@kennedy-center.org.

ACCESS FOR SUPPORTERS

NASM states that many of its tour guides are trained to support people with access needs. If you want to take a self-guided tour or to attend walk-in programs at the museum, you can go to the visitor center when you arrive, and they'll assist you and your supporter. However, if you have specific access issues, I'd advise that you contact the museum before you arrive. Call 202 633 2214.

Contact **SNMNH** if you or your supporter have particular access needs that can't be addressed by its main programs or services. Call 202 633 5238 or email NMNHAccessibility@si.edu. If you are visiting as a family, the museum also has the Q?rius areas that have largely accessible exhibits and educational technologies for children and teenagers.

The National Gallery offers a program of workshops called the Art of Care for Medical Professionals for visitors working in medicine, support workers, or others who provide support. This program teaches visitors how to support people with access needs through artworks, such as those at the gallery. To get onto this program or for further information, call 202 842 6905 or email access@nga.gov.

Not all information on specific access issues and issues at the **NMAAH& C** are advertised through its regular calendars, brochures, or website. So, contact the Smithsonian Accessibility Office before you visit; email access@si.edu. In addition, for this museum and all the other Smithsonian museums discussed earlier, visit the main **Smithsonian** access website for specialist advice and information on specialist needs, or on visiting with families, as a group, or as a supporter: www.si.edu/accessibility.

For specialist information about accessibility at **Kennedy Center**, call 202 416 8727 or email access@kennedy-center.org. The center advertises that it can do its best to support access issues that are not advertised through its regular brochures, calendars, or website.

Notes

1. INTRODUCTION

1. United Nations Educational, Scientific, and Cultural Organization, "The Right to Culture," 1, www.unesco.org/new/en/kabul/culture/programmes-and-projects/the-right-to-culture/
2. Simon Hayhoe, *Arts, Culture, and Blindness* (Amherst, NY: Teneo Press, 2008).
3. Simon Hayhoe, *Blind Visitor Experiences at Art Museums* (Lanham, MD: Rowman & Littlefield, 2017).
4. Simon Hayhoe, *Cultural Heritage, Ageing, Disability, and Identity* (New York: Routledge, 2019).
5. Ibid.

ACCESS NEEDS

1. See Simon Hayhoe, *Philosophy as Disability & Exclusion* (Charlotte, NC: Information Age Publishing, 2016).
2. See Hayhoe, *Blind Visitor Experiences at Art Museums*; Hayhoe, *Cultural Heritage, Ageing, Disability, and Identity*; Hayhoe, "Expanding Our Vision of Museum Education and Perception," *Harvard Educational Review* 83, no. 1 (2013): 67–86; Viktor Lowenfeld, "Psycho-Aesthetic Implications of the Art of the Blind," *The Journal of Aesthetics and Art Criticism* 10, no. 1 (1951): 1–9; Robert J. Saunders, "The Contributions of Viktor Lowenfeld to Art Education," *Studies in Art Education* 2, no. 2 (1960): 6–15; John M. Kennedy, "What Can We Learn about Pictures from the Blind?" *American Scientist* 71, no. 1 (1983): 19–26; Kennedy, "How the Blind Draw," *Scientific American* 276, no. 1 (1997): 76–81; Kennedy, *Drawing and the Blind* (New Haven, CT: Yale University Press, 1993); Lee Campbell, "You Don't Need Eyes to See, You Need Vision," *Journal of Pedagogic Development* 7, no. 3 (2017): 3–12.
3. For example, see Hayhoe, *Blind Visitor Experiences at Art Museums*; Hayhoe, *Cultural Heritage, Ageing, Disability, and Identity*.

2. HEARING LOSS

1. NIDCD, "Quick Statistics about Hearing," 2016, accessed December 6, 2018, www.nidcd.nih.gov/health/statistics/quick-statistics-hearing.

2. Hayhoe, *Cultural Heritage, Ageing, Disability, and Identity.*

3. Hayhoe, "Expanding Our Vision," 67–86; Hayhoe, *Blind Visitor Experiences at Art Museums*; Hayhoe, *Cultural Heritage, Ageing, Disability, and Identity.*

4. Hayhoe, *Blind Visitor Experiences at Art Museums.*

5. Francis B. Colavita, "Human Sensory Dominance," *Perception & Psychophysics* 16, no. 2 (1974): 409–12; Charles Spence, "Explaining the Colavita Visual Dominance Effect," *Progress in Brain Research* 176, no. 0 (2009): 245–58.

6. US Government, "ADA General Guidelines," 2010, accessed December 6, 2018, http://www.ada.gov/regs2010/2010ADAStandards/2010ADAStandards.pdf.

7. Ibid.

3. SIGHT LOSS

1. Scott C. LaBarre, "Marrakesh Express Rolling Home," *Voice of the Nation's Blind* (October 2, 2018), nfb.org/blog/marrakesh-express-rolling-home.

2. Rohit Varma et al. "Visual Impairment and Blindness in Adults in the United States," *JAMA Ophthalmology* 134, no. 7 (2016): 802–9.

3. Ibid.

4. Simon Hayhoe, "The Effects of Late Arts Education on Adults with Early Visual Disabilities," *Educational Research & Evaluation* 6, no. 3 (2000): 229–49; Hayhoe, *Arts, Culture, and Blindness*; Hayhoe, *Blind Visitor Experiences at Art Museums*; Madhumita Bhattacharya, Nada Mach, and Mahnaz Moallum, eds., *Emerging Technologies in Learning: Impact on Cognition and Culture* (AACE, 2011); George Ghinea, Frederic Andres, and Stephen Gulliver, *Multiple Sensorial Media Advances and Applications: New Developments in MulSeMedia* (Information Science Reference, 2011).

5. Bhattacharya, Mach, and Moallum, *Emerging Technologies*; Ghinea, Adres, and Gulliver, *Multiple Sensorial.*

6. Oliver Sacks, *The Island of the Colour-Blind and Cycad Island* (New York: Pan Macmillan, 1997); Hayhoe, *Arts, Culture, and Blindness.*

7. John M. Kennedy and Igor Juricevic, "Foreshortening, Convergence and Drawings from a Blind Adult," *Perception* 35, no. 6 (2006): 847–51; Hayhoe, *Blind Visitor Experiences at Art Museums.*

8. John M. Hull, *Touching the Rock* (New York: Vintage, 1992).

9. Hayhoe, *Philosophy as Disability & Exclusion.*

10. Georgina Kleege, *Sight Unseen* (New Haven, CT: Yale University Press, 1999).

11. Georgina Kleege, *More Than Meets the Eye* (Oxford: Oxford University Press, 2017).

4. LEARNING DIFFICULTIES AND MEMORY LOSS

1. Jack D. Maser and Hagop S. Akiskal, "Spectrum Concepts in Major Mental Disorders," *Psychiatric Clinics* 25, no. 4 (2002): xi–xiii.

2. Alan Baddeley et al., "The Brain Decade in Debate," *Brazilian Journal of Medical and Biological Research* 33, no. 9 (2000): 993–1002.

3. John Locke, *The Clarendon Edition of the Works of John Locke* (Oxford: Clarendon Press, 1979).

4. Simon Hayhoe, "Classical Philosophies on Blindness and Cross-Modal Transfer, 1688–2003," in *The Routledge Handbook of Visual Impairment: Social and Cultural Research*, ed. John Ravenscroft (Abingdon, UK: Routledge, 2018), 227–37.

5. Jean Piaget, "Part I: Cognitive Development in Children: Piaget Development and Learning," *Journal of Research in Science Teaching* 2, no. 3 (1964): 176–86.

6. S. H. Horowitz, J. Rowe, and M. C. Whittaker, *The State of Learning Disabilities* (New York: National Center for Learning Disabilities, 2017), 1.

7. Peter Crosta, "What to Know about Down Syndrome," *Medical News Today*, December 6, 2017.

8. CDC, "Data and Statistics on Down Syndrome," accessed July 17, 2019, www.cdc.gov/ncbddd/birthdefects/downsyndrome/data.html.

9. Lev Vygotsky, *Mind in Society* (Cambridge, MA: Harvard University Press, 1980).

10. Mental Health Foundation, "Easy Read," accessed July 17, 2018, www.mentalhealth.org.uk/learning-disabilities/a-to-z/e/easy-read.

11. Asit B. Biswas et al., "Obesity in People with Learning Disabilities," *Nursing Times* 106, no. 31 (2010): 16–18.

12. Learning Disabilities Association of America, "Related Disorders of a Learning Disability," accessed July 17, 2019, ldaamerica.org/what-you-should-know-about-related-disorders-of-learning-disability/.

13. Ibid.

14. Krishnagopal Dharani, *The Biology of Thought* (London: Academic Press, 2014).

15. Alzheimer's Association, "What Is Dementia?" accessed July 22, 2019, www.alz.org/alzheimers-dementia/what-is-dementia.

16. Sharon Manship and Eleni Hatzidimitriadou, *A Qualitative Evaluation of Psychosocial Outcomes* (Canterbury: Canterbury Christ Church University, 2015).

17. Museum of Modern Art, *The MoMA Alzheimer's Project* (New York: MoMA, 2008).

18. Ibid.

5. MOBILE TECHNOLOGIES AND CULTURAL PLACES

1. Simon Hayhoe, "Inclusive Technical Capital in the Twenty-First Century," in *Inclusion, Equity and Access for Individuals with Disabilities* (Singapore: Palgrave Macmillan, 2019), 223–41.

2. Hayhoe et al., "Developing Inclusive Technical Capital beyond the Disabled Students' Allowance in England," *Social Inclusion* 3, no. 6 (2015): 29–41.

3. Hayhoe, "A Philosophy of Inclusive Technology," in *Proceedings of EDULEARN14: Education and New Learning Technologies* (Valencia: IATED, 2014), 7579–87.

4. Hayhoe et al., "Evaluation of a Collaborative Photography Workshop," in *2017 14th IEEE Annual Consumer Communications & Networking Conference* (Las Vegas, NV: IEEE, 2017), 1077–82.

5. Hayhoe, "A Pedagogical Evaluation of Accessible Settings," in *INTED 2015 Proceedings* (Valencia: IATED, 2015), 2220–28.

TWELVE CITIES

1. Simon Hayhoe, *Cultural Heritage, Ageing, Disability, and Identity*.

2. See, for example, Amber Pariona, "The Most Visited Cities in the US," *World Atlas*, accessed August 20, 2019, www.worldatlas.com/articles/the-most-visited-cities-in-the-us.html.

3. I've also faced the problem of leaving out some popular cities when making these choices, as I couldn't find enough accessible places in some cities. In this book, I don't name these cities, but it is interesting to note that even in 2019, big popular cities still don't place huge importance on accessibility.

8. CHICAGO, ILLINOIS

1. R. David Edmunds, "Chicago in the Middle Ground," *The Encyclopedia of Chicago—Historical Society*, accessed February 26, 2020, http://www.encyclopedia.chicagohistory.org/pages/254.html; Perry R. Duis and Cathlyn Schallhorn, "Chicago (People)," *Encyclopædia Britannica*, accessed February 26, 2020, https://www.britannica.com/place/Chicago/People.

2. Cathlyn Schallhorn and Perry R. Duis, "Chicago," *Encyclopædia Britannica*, accessed February 26, 2020, https://www.britannica.com/place/Chicago/History#ref257578; and Loomis Mayfield, "Government, City of Chicago," *The Encyclopedia of Chicago—Historical Society*, accessed February 26, 2020, http://www.encyclopedia.chicagohistory.org/pages/532.html.

11. LOS ANGELES, CALIFORNIA

1. Karen R. Lawrence, "President's Welcome," *The Huntington*, accessed February 26, 2020, https://www.huntington.org/welcome.

13. NEW YORK CITY, NEW YORK

1. Chaim Gross, *The Technique of Wood Sculpture* (McBride, BC, Canada: Vista House, 1957).

2. Chelangat Faith, "The Largest Art Museums in the United States," *WorldAtlas*, August 14, 2017, accessed November 24, 2019, worldatlas.com/articles/the-largest-art-museums-in-the-united-states.html.

3. Simon Hayhoe, *Blind Visitor Experiences at Art Museums*.

15. SAN FRANCISCO, CALIFORNIA

1. Kenneth Lamott and Gladys Cox Hansen, "San Francisco," *Encyclopædia Britannica*, accessed November 24, 2019, https://www.britannica.com/place/San-Francisco-California.

16. SEATTLE, WASHINGTON

1. Gregory Lewis McNamee, "Seattle," *Encyclopædia Britannica*, 2019, accessed November 24, 2019, https://www.britannica.com/place/Seattle-Washington.

2. Seattle Art Museum, *Seattle Art Museum Annual Report 2016–2017* (Seattle: Seattle Art Museum, 2018).

3. Alan Stein, "Museum of History & Industry (MOHAI)," HistoryLink.org Essay 3682, 2002, accessed October 1, 2019, https://www.historylink.org/File/3682.

4. Edward Rothstein, "A Place Comfortable with Boeing, Anarchists and 'Frasier': Museum of History & Industry Reopens in Seattle," *New York Times*, December 28, 2012.

5. Delaney Berreth, "Blast from the Past: The Fascinating History of Pacific Science Center's Architecture," *Pacific North West Magazine*, October 16, 2017.

6. Kirstin Matthews and Vivian Ho, "The Grand Impact of the Gates Foundation," *EMBO Reports* 9, no. 5 (2008): 409–12.

7. Frank Catalano, "Gates Foundation's Seattle Exhibit Center Gets Refreshed with a New Name, More Interaction," *Geek Wire*, November 25, 2017.

8. National Park Service, "Paramount Theatre," accessed October 1, 2019, https://www.nps.gov/nr/travel/seattle/s14.htm.

17. WASHINGTON, DC

1. Smithsonian Institute, "Visitor Stats," accessed October 1, 2019, www.si.edu/newsdesk/about/stats.

Bibliography

Alzheimer's Association. "What Is Dementia?" Accessed July 22, 2019. https://www.alz.org/alzheimers-dementia/what-is-dementia.

Baddeley, Alan, Orlando Bueno, Larry Cahill, Joaquin M. Fuster, I. Izquierdo, James L. McGaugh, R. G. M. Morris, et al. "The Brain Decade in Debate: I. Neurobiology of Learning and Memory." *Brazilian Journal of Medical and Biological Research* 33, no. 9 (2000): 993–1002.

Berreth, Delaney. "Blast from the Past: The Fascinating History of Pacific Science Center's Architecture." *Pacific North West Magazine*, October 16, 2017.

Biswas, Asit B., Arshya Vahabzadeh, Tracy Hobbs, and James M. Healy. "Obesity in People with Learning Disabilities: Possible Causes and Reduction Interventions." *Nursing Times* 106, no. 31 (2010): 16–18.

Campbell, Lee. "You Don't Need Eyes to See, You Need Vision: Performative Pedagogy, Technology and Teaching Art to Students with Vision Impairment." *Journal of Pedagogic Development* 7, no. 3 (2017): 3–12.

Catalano, Frank. "Gates Foundation's Seattle Exhibit Center Gets Refreshed with a New Name, More Interaction." *Geek Wire*, November 25, 2017.

CDC. "Data and Statistics on Down Syndrome." Accessed July 17, 2019. https://www.cdc.gov/ncbddd/birthdefects/downsyndrome/data.html.

Colavita, Francis B. "Human Sensory Dominance." *Perception & Psychophysics* 16, no. 2 (1974): 409–12.

Crosta, Peter. "What to Know about Down Syndrome." *Medical News Today*, December 6, 2017. https://www.medicalnewstoday.com/articles/145554.

Dharani, Krishnagopal. *The Biology of Thought: A Neuronal Mechanism in the Generation of Thought—A New Molecular Model.* London: Academic Press, 2014.

Duis, Perry R., and Cathlyn Schallhorn. "Chicago." *Encyclopædia Britannica.* November 14, 2019. Accessed November 18, 2019. https://www.britannica.com/place/Chicago.

Faith, Chelangat. "The Largest Art Museums in the United States." *WorldAtlas*, August 14, 2017. Accessed November 24, 2019. https://www.worldatlas.com/articles/the-largest-art-museums-in-the-united-states.html.

Gross, Chaim. *The Technique of Wood Sculpture.* McBride, BC, Canada: Vista House, 1957.

Hayhoe, Simon. "A Pedagogical Evaluation of Accessible Settings in Google's Android and Apple's IoS Mobile Operating Systems and Native Apps Using the SAMR Model of Educational Technology and an Educational Model of Technical Capital." In *INTED2015 Proceedings*, 2220–28. Valencia: IATED, 2015.

Hayhoe, Simon. "A Philosophy of Inclusive Technology for People with Special Needs, and Its Application in a Course Using Mobile Computing Devices for Undergraduates at the London School of Economics." In *Proceedings of EDULEARN14: Education and New Learning Technologies*, 7579–87. Valencia: IATED, 2014.

Hayhoe, Simon. *Arts, Culture, and Blindness : A Study of Blind Students in the Visual Arts.* Amherst, NY: Teneo Press, 2008.

Hayhoe, Simon. *Blind Visitor Experiences at Art Museums.* Lanham, MD: Rowman & Littlefield, 2017.

Hayhoe, Simon. "Classical Philosophies on Blindness and Cross-Modal Transfer, 1688–2003." In *The Routledge Handbook of Visual Impairment: Social and Cultural Research*, edited by John Ravenscroft, 227–37. Abingdon, UK: Routledge, 2018.

Hayhoe, Simon. *Cultural Heritage, Ageing, Disability, and Identity: Practice, and the Development of Inclusive Capital.* New York: Routledge, 2019.

Hayhoe, Simon. "Expanding Our Vision of Museum Education and Perception: An Analysis of Three Case Studies of Independent Blind Arts Learners." *Harvard Educational Review* 83, no. 1 (2013): 67–86.

Hayhoe, Simon. *Grounded Theory and Disability Studies: An Investigation into Legacies of Blindness.* Amherst, NY: Cambria Press, 2012.

Hayhoe, Simon. "Inclusive Technical Capital in the Twenty-First Century." In *Inclusion, Equity and Access for Individuals with Disabilities*, 223–41. Singapore: Palgrave Macmillan, 2019.

Hayhoe, Simon. *Philosophy as Disability & Exclusion: The Development of Theories on Blindness, Touch and the Arts in England, 1688–2010.* Charlotte, NC: Information Age Publishing, 2016.

Hayhoe, Simon. "The Effects of Late Arts Education on Adults with Early Visual Disabilities." *Educational Research & Evaluation* 6, no. 3 (2000): 229–49.

Hayhoe, Simon. "The Need for Inclusive Accessible Technologies for Students with Disabilities and Learning Difficulties." In L. Burke, *Research, Reflections & Arguments on Teaching & Learning in a Digital Age*, 257–74. Melton, UK: John Catt Educational Publishing, 2014.

Hayhoe, Simon, Carla Tonin, and Graziella Lunardi. "A Model of Inclusive Capital for Analysis of Non-Economic Human Capital." Poster presented at *Decent Work, Equity and Inclusion, Padova, Italy* 5, no. 10 (2017): 17–27.

Hayhoe, Simon, Kris Roger, Sebastiaan Eldritch-Böersen, and Linda Kelland. "Developing Inclusive Technical Capital beyond the Disabled Students' Allowance in England." *Social Inclusion* 3, no. 6 (2015): 29–41.

Hayhoe, Simon, Noemi Pena-Sanchez, and Karl Bentley. "Evaluation of a Collaborative Photography Workshop Using the iPad 2 as an Accessible Technology for Participants Who Are Blind, Visually Impaired and Sighted Working Collaboratively." In *2017 14th IEEE Annual Consumer Communications & Networking Conference (CCNC)*, 1077–82. Las Vegas, NV: IEEE, 2017.

Horowitz, S. H., J. Rawe, and M. C. Whittaker. *The State of Learning Disabilities: Understanding the 1 in 5.* New York: National Center for Learning Disabilities, 2017.

Hull, John M. *Touching the Rock : An Experience of Blindness.* New York: Vintage, 1992.

Kennedy, John M. *Drawing & the Blind: Pictures to Touch.* New Haven, CT: Yale University Press, 1993.

Kennedy, John M. "How the Blind Draw." *Scientific American* 276, no. 1 (1997): 76–81.

Kennedy, John M. "What Can We Learn about Pictures from the Blind? Blind People Unfamiliar with Pictures Can Draw in a Universally Recognizable Outline Style." *American Scientist* 71, no. 1 (1983): 19–26.

Kennedy, John M., and Igor Juricevic. "Foreshortening, Convergence and Drawings from a Blind Adult." *Perception* 35, no. 6 (2006): 847–51.

Kleege, Georgina. *More Than Meets the Eye: What Blindness Brings to Art.* Oxford: Oxford University Press, 2017.

Kleege, Georgina. *Sight Unseen.* New Haven, CT: Yale University Press, 1999.

LaBarre, Scott C. "Marrakesh Express Rolling Home." *Voice of the Nation's Blind.* October 2, 2018. https://nfb.org/blog/marrakesh-express-rolling-home.

Lamott, Kenneth, and Gladys Cox Hansen. "San Francisco." *Encyclopædia Britannica*. 2019. Accessed November 24, 2019. https://www.britannica.com/place/San-Francisco-California.

Learning Disabilities Association of America. "Related Disorders of a Learning Disability: What You Should Know." Accessed July 17, 2019. https://ldaamerica.org/what-you-should-know-about-related-disorders-of-learning-disability/.

Lewis McNamee, Gregory. "Seattle." *Encyclopædia Britannica*. 2019. Accessed November 24, 2019. https://www.britannica.com/place/Seattle-Washington.

Locke, John. *The Clarendon Edition of the Works of John Locke: An Essay concerning Human Understanding*. Oxford: Clarendon Press, 1979.

Lowenfeld, Viktor. "Psycho-Aesthetic Implications of the Art of the Blind." *The Journal of Aesthetics and Art Criticism* 10, no. 1 (1951): 1–9.

Manship, Sharon, and Eleni Hatzidimitriadou. *A Qualitative Evaluation of Psychosocial Outcomes of the Creative Communications Pilot Project for People with Dementia*. Canterbury: Canterbury Christ Church University, 2015.

Maser, Jack D., and Hagop S. Akiskal. "Spectrum Concepts in Major Mental Disorders." *Psychiatric Clinics* 25, no. 4 (2002): xi–xiii.

Matthews, Kirstin, and Vivian Ho. "The Grand Impact of the Gates Foundation." *EMBO Reports* 9, no. 5 (2008): 409–12.

Mental Health Foundation. "Easy Read." Accessed July 17, 2018. https://www.mentalhealth.org.uk/learning-disabilities/a-to-z/e/easy-read.

Museum of Modern Art. *The MoMA Alzheimer's Project: Making Art Accessible to People with Dementia, A Guide for Museums*. New York: MoMA, 2008.

National Institute on Deafness and Other Communication Disorders. "Quick Statistics about Hearing." 2016. Accessed December 6, 2018. https://www.nidcd.nih.gov/health/statistics/quick-statistics-hearing.

National Park Service. "Paramount Theatre." Accessed October 1, 2019. https://www.nps.gov/nr/travel/seattle/s14.htm.

Pariona, Amber. "The Most Visited Cities in the US." *WorldAtlas*. Accessed August 20, 2019. https://www.worldatlas.com/articles/the-most-visited-cities-in-the-us.html.

Piaget, Jean. "Part I: Cognitive Development in Children: Piaget Development and Learning." *Journal of Research in Science Teaching* 2, no. 3 (1964): 176–86.

Rothstein, Edward. "A Place Comfortable with Boeing, Anarchists and 'Frasier': Museum of History & Industry Reopens in Seattle." *New York Times*, December 28, 2012.

Sacks, Oliver. *The Island of the Colour-Blind and Cycad Island*. New York: Pan Macmillan, 1997.

Saunders, Robert J. "The Contributions of Viktor Lowenfeld to Art Education; Part I: Early Influences on His Thought." *Studies in Art Education* 2, no. 1 (1960): 6–15.

Seattle Art Museum. *Seattle Art Museum Annual Report, 2016–2017, July 1, 2016 through June 30, 2017*. Seattle: Seattle Art Museum, 2018.

Smithsonian Institute. "Visitor Stats." Accessed October 1, 2019. https://www.si.edu/newsdesk/about/stats.

Somekh, Bridget, Herbert Altrichter, and Peter Posch. *Teachers Investigate Their Work: An Introduction to the Methods of Action Research*. New York: Routledge, 1995.

Spence, Charles. "Explaining the Colavita Visual Dominance Effect." *Progress in Brain Research* 176, no. 0 (2009): 245–58.

Stein, Alan. "Museum of History & Industry (MOHAI)." HistoryLink.org Essay 3682. 2002. Accessed October 1, 2019. https://www.historylink.org/File/3682.

United Nations Educational, Scientific and Cultural Organization. "The Right to Culture." Paris: UNESCO, 2019.

US Government. "ADA General Guidelines." 2010. Accessed December 6, 2018. http://www.ada.gov/regs2010/2010ADAStandards/2010ADAStandards.pdf.

Varma, Rohit, Thasarat S. Vajaranant, Bruce Burkemper, Shuang Wu, Mina Torres, Chunyi Hsu, Farzana Choudhury, and Roberta McKean-Cowdin. "Visual Impairment and Blindness in Adults in the United States: Demographic and Geographic Variations from 2015 to 2050." *JAMA Ophthalmology* 134, no. 7 (2016): 802–9.

Vygotsky, Lev Semenovich. *Mind in Society: The Development of Higher Psychological Processes*. Cambridge, MA: Harvard University Press, 1980.

Index

About the Author

Simon Hayhoe is the author of six books on art education and museum access for people with disabilities and is also an educational advisor for the World Health Organization. His current work focuses on inclusive mobile technologies, and he has just completed a European project investigating the use of mobile technologies by disabled people in museums and monuments. Hayhoe has won numerous awards in his field, including a Fulbright Award and a Fellowship of the Metropolitan Museum of Art, and he has presented his work at major museums and colleges in the US, Russia, UK, Spain, Singapore, Belgium, and Italy. Beyond work and writing, Hayhoe lives in a beautiful town on a hill with his wife and two children, close to where he was born and raised.